THE MARIONETTE ACTOR

RALPH CHESSÉ

George Mason University Press
Fairfax, Virginia

Copyright © 1987 by
George Mason University Press

4400 University Drive
Fairfax, VA 22030

Printed in the United States of America

British Cataloging in Publication Information Available

Distributed by arrangement with
University Publishing Associates, Inc.

4720 Boston Way
Lanham, MD 20706

3 Henrietta Street
London WC2E 8LU England

Library of Congress Cataloging-in-Publication Data

Chesse, Ralph.
    The marionette actor.

    Bibliography: p.
    1. Chesse, Ralph.   2. Puppeteers—United States—
Biography.   3. Puppets and puppet-plays.   I. Title.
PN1982.C44A3   1987   791.5'3'0924 [B]   87-413
ISBN 0-8026-0011-5 (alk. paper)
ISBN 0-8026-0012-3 (alk. paper : pbk.)

All George Mason University Press books are produced on acid-free
paper which exceeds the minimum standards set by the National
Historical Publications and Records Commission.

DEDICATION

To Bruce, Lettie, Dion, and all those
who have worked with me over the years
bringing life to the marionette.

CONTENTS

Foreword

For almost sixty years, the Chessé Marionettes have entertained California audiences in theatres and on television. How fortunate we were that Ralph, with his talents as actor and artist and filled with inspiration from Edward Gordon Craig, came to San Francisco in the 1920s and began to produce marionette shows of unusual quality. His productions of "Hamlet," "Emperor Jones," "Don Juan," "Macbeth," and "The Crock of Gold" have contributed greatly to the recognition of puppetry as a theater art to be appreciated by adult intellectual audiences. His productions for children were also marked with dignity and a respect for the audience and for the work itself.

How I wish I had been an adult in the late 1920s and early 1930s so I could have seen the early shows. My parents and their contemporaries later filled my adolescent ears with flowing descriptions of those productions. My earliest memory of any puppet show was the Chessé "Alice in Wonderland." I vividly remember the atmosphere of a theatre filled with children and adults watching Alice and the Red Queen running to keep in place. About the same time, I was given a monkey hand puppet at nursery school which I attended with Dion Chessé (the eldest of Ralph and Jo's children). It is no wonder with those first exposures that my involvement with puppetry has been so pervasive.

Even though I was incredibly fortunate hearing some of Chessé's anecdotes, ideas, and theories in the years that I apprenticed and worked for and with him in puppetry, there were many more experiences untold because of interruptions or lack of opportunity. At last through this book, we all will be able to glimpse a fascinating creative and productive life. I hope the reader will appreciate the scope of the treasure he or she is being offered.

The reader will not get from this book one thing I wish I could share with everyone who opens it. It was a very special gift, one that few others received. Some here in California could enjoy Ralph's work as an actor or puppet master, many have appreciated his paintings and murals even though a number have not had the privilege of knowing the artist. Even those who took part in his productions or classes were not as fortunate as I was in receiving his continued guidance. For fourteen years, Ralph was my teacher and mentor. He patiently inspired, influenced, instructed, and encouraged my work and yet his way of supervising and instructing allowed me to evolve my own style, identity, and philosophy of puppetry. This is all the more extraordinary when a teacher has such strong theories and conceptions of his own. I am not sure Ralph is aware of this very special faculty. It is one more facet of an unique talent. We who love and respect Ralph Chessé are delighted that through the publication of this book you will also have the opportunity to explore his theories and experiences.

Lettie Connell Schubert
June 1986

Acknowledgements

I would like to express my thanks to all those who have, in one way or another, made possible the publication of this book. I am especially indebted to the encouragement and enthusiasm of Lorraine Brown and Barbara Smith of the Institute on the Federal Theatre Project and New Deal Culture of George Mason University, for bringing about the documentation of my work. A special thanks to Joann Meredith for her excellent editing and typing of the manuscript, to Jean Burn in her persistence in urging me on to the completion of this project, and to Lettie Connell, Louis Mahlman, Alan Cook, and Joan Simms-Morgenstern for their faith in me. I am indebted to my children, Dion, Bruce, and Renee, in their dedicated support in all my marionette projects. To Dion, especially, who was responsible for putting much of the book together. And, finally, to Vernon Gras of GMU Press, who is responsible for bringing this all about.

R.A.C.

Introduction

When I began puppetry more than fifty years ago, I did not start out to make marionettes. Inspired by the theories of Gordon Craig, I intended to make an instrument of theatre, a surrogate which would serve my purpose as an actor. I contemplated the philosophy behind the diminutive characters of wood. I attempted to understand my own feelings about them and, at the same time, to understand the approach of other puppeteers who had gone before me. With these considerations in mind, I began writing this book.

So much of the literature of puppetry has either chronicled its history or explained the processes of construction and production, both important aspects. However, a significant issue has been overlooked: that is, the dramatic theatre which we have always accepted as belonging to actors of flesh and blood. I believe the marionette can take its place in the theatre with the best of these actors and make a contribution to theatre form which only it can provide.

All marionettes and puppets are not works of art, however interesting they may be, yet they can afford the greatest stimulation to the imagination when their production is approached as a creative problem by the artist. Their growth and development depend on the artist and the actor, and it is to them I offer the contents of this book.

ONE

The best actors in the world, either for tragedy, comedy, history, pastoral, pastoral–comical, historical–pastoral, tragical–historical, tragical–comical–historical–pastoral, scene individable, or poem unlimited; Seneca cannot be too heavy, nor Plautus too light. For the law of writ and the liberty, these are the only men.

— Shakespeare, *Hamlet* – II:2

The small theatre back of the little lending library at 718 Montgomery Street in San Francisco was buzzing with excitement. The makeshift benches were filled with a mixture of news writers, art critics, drama critics, poets, artists from the Montgomery Block at the corner, musicians, devotees of Shakespeare, and the cream of the intelligentsia whose curiosities had been aroused by the news announcements that the immortal *Hamlet* was to be presented with marionettes. They expected little more than a burlesque from an ambitious crew of amateur actors; and with marionettes, it had to be for a laugh.

As the theatre darkened and the lights came up on the front curtains, the strains of a Wagnerian overture came from a record player backstage. A hush of expectancy came over the audience as the curtains parted revealing a dimly lighted stage. Claudius was seated on his throne next to Gertrude. The King was bathed in a blood–red spotlight while the Queen's light was a cool blue–green complementing the red. There were Polonius, Ophelia, Laertes, the guards to the right and left of them, and to one side, off center, sitting alone, all in black, was Hamlet. On the bridge above, we tensely held the life–giving controls to the characters below.

The silence was broken as Max McCarthy spoke for the King: "Though yet of Hamlet our dear brother's death the memory be green . . . ." We were on. I trembled a little and the vibrations went down through the strings as Hamlet answered with a slight movement of the head: "A little more than kin and less than kind." Checking

1

my emotion, I concentrated on the figure below. The marionette was performing its role beautifully; I could feel the attention of the audience. I lost myself in the poetic reading of the lines and felt I was on that stage playing the part.

Instead of giving away the Ghost with the usual opening on the castle's platform, I had the King open the play with Scene II. The announcement of the Ghost's appearance was revealed by Horatio, Marcellus, and Bernardo, who come to tell Hamlet what they have seen. In this way, a suspense was created so that when the huge, green shadow of Hamlet's father loomed in the next scene, it came as a complete surprise to the audience. And it worked. Bursts of applause followed the closing of each curtain and the excitement backstage rose to a fever pitch. There were no slips; the company did very well, and I felt that in spite of the simplicity and abbreviated version of the play I presented (I also eliminated Rosencrantz and Guildenstern), the audience accepted my Hamlet as an actor, not just as a marionette. During the intermission, the hub–bub indicated that these small wooden actors had found their enthusiasts.

By using dramatic lighting that painted the simple neutral settings with strong color, backing some of the scenes with appropriate mood music, and manipulating the jointed figures with a minimum of gestures, the characters came alive. Combined with a moving reading of the lines, we created something comparable to the performances of live actors. The audience was moved, and, as an actor, I proved to myself I could derive as great a satisfaction by using a marionette to play Hamlet as I could by performing the role myself. I was able to control a scene from the bridge as an orchestra conductor controls his musicians' rendition of a score. The great soliloquies, the Queen's closet scene, the Gravediggers' scene, which was the comedy relief, contrasting the tragedy of Ophelia's burial and the final duel scene with Laertes, all came off as planned.

The audience never realized that much of what they thought they saw was actually filled in by their own imaginations. Imagination, which must always be exercised by those watching a theatrical performance, was here strained to the utmost, thus complementing our efforts entirely. The Gravedigger throwing out the bones from Ophelia's grave was not played as a trick; it was believed. When Hamlet dropped his hand into the grave and came up with the skull of Yorick, the audience did not gasp but accepted it as a very natural occurrence. In the duel scene, we faked the exchange of swords by merely dropping them to the floor and covering the action with the two marionettes struggling to gain possession of the poisoned one. The viewers never questioned it. We created an illusion that made the small actors grow to a gigantic size. Everything they said and did within that proscenium was in proportion.

After the performance, when we invited the audience backstage to examine the marionettes, they were amazed by their small size. Some described in detail certain things which they believed they had seen, the actual carrying out of which would have been impossible. Their enthusiasm extended far beyond anything for which I had hoped. I was elated as was the rest of the company including Blanding Sloan, who initially took the credit for presenting the classic in this new form. The next day the newspapers and magazines appeared lauding our efforts and achievements; photographs were spread across the pages with review columns and feature stories praising the new *Hamlet*. The marionettes were headline news.

TWO

How did it all begin? I suppose that every experience, everything I ever did before that opening night of *Hamlet* contributed in some way to that first performance.

My first taste of Shakespeare came in grammar school where I was called upon to read speeches from *The Merchant of Venice, Julius Caesar*, and *As You Like It*. At age thirteen, I was hooked. I saw my first performance of *The Merchant of Venice* with Robert Mantell playing Shylock—from then on I wanted to be a Shakespearean actor. I memorized all of the great speeches and recited them to anyone who would listen.

At age eighteen, playing in a church musical, I put on greasepaint for the first time. I felt a great thrill appearing before an audience, although in a silly character part. Nevertheless, it was theatre—new and exciting to me.

I also loved to paint and draw and was determined to exercise that talent as well. So I went to the Chicago Art Institute for awhile but found that wasn't the answer. Returning to New Orleans where I was born, I got into amateur theatricals even working a few weeks with a fly-by-night stock company. I felt very professional. However, they moved on leaving me behind, reasoning that because of my small size, I would not be of much use to them. I then went to *Le Petit Theatre du Vieux Carré* in the French Quarter. Mark Antony, their stage designer, needed a helper to paint scenery and props. Also, the director found they could use me as a makeup man. These two positions, in addition to playing small parts occasionally, brought together my painting and acting talents. I thought I had found what I was looking for.

I also had occasion to go on stage as an extra when Robert Mantell's Shakespearean Company came to town. It was thrilling to be on stage watching and hearing that fine old actor recite the soliloquies in *Julius Caesar*. I was nearing the satisfaction of my first ambition.

In 1923, I came out to California, landed first in Hollywood where I intended to find work as an extra, but instead took a job as a timekeeper on a painting crew. Although the job lasted only six months, it offered a bit more security than working as an extra. I then decided to try San Francisco where I had a few friends.

It was there in 1924 that I first met Blanding Sloan, who was conducting a class in stage design. I joined his class, and we became friends. He had a hilltop studio on Greenwich and Polk Streets which consisted of two old refugee shacks surrounded by tall eucalyptus trees and without benefit of plumbing. His wife, Mildred Taylor, and he lived in a more elegant apartment in Chinatown.

Blanding told me a little about his early life. When he was very young, he had left his home in Texas to "discover the world." While hopping a freight train, he slipped and fell under the wheels, losing one of his legs below the knee. I had noticed a slight limp in his walk but was unaware that he was wearing an artificial leg until he joked about it, striking his leg with a loud thump. This disability did not slow him down; he was as swift and agile as anyone with two good legs. He was a small man: gentle, quiet and soft spoken, with a slight Texas accent. Many young artists were drawn to him and came to his studio to share the working atmosphere he created along with the use of his tools and etching press. They became involved in all of Blanding's creative interests: drawing, etching, block prints, painting, and especially puppets.

Inspired by this atmosphere, I came under the spell and was initiated into puppetry. I moved into the shack with two other young artists: one a wild, bushy–haired Italian, Salvatore Macri, and the other Richard Soloman, a middle–aged Englishman, weaver, and health food cultist, who had his loom set up in the front room where he wove and incessantly talked of politics, usually cursing the "bloody economic system." I was very happy with my life there among artists until Blanding decided to turn the shack into a marionette theatre, so I had to move out and find other lodgings.

Blanding cut through the ceiling of my former bedroom, built a stage on the lower floor, and used the upper level as a marionette bridge. I continued coming to the studio and became one of the puppeteers for *Rastus Plays Pirate*, a play Blanding had written and with which he opened his Shack Theatre.

As an actor and painter, I was fascinated by the potential of the marionette as a dramatic art form. I learned to manipulate to my own reading of lines and found a new use for my earlier theatre training.

Although Blanding was a fine craftsman and wood carver, he was not a puppeteer and only occasionally climbed up on the bridge. He recognized my acting talent and encouraged me to continue in puppetry, as he did all the young artists who came around, always stressing the importance of artistic freedom.

While in San Francisco, I made my living by teaching batik in a department store. I saved my money and planned my next move: this time, New York City.

Broadway was a magnet to me as it is to most young actors and theatre people. I was a bit overwhelmed and determined more than ever to get into it one way or another. Living in Greenwich Village was another dream come true.

I had taken a set of costume drawings with settings for a production of *Hamlet*. With these, I made the rounds of the producers and designers on and off Broadway, and on the strength of these, I landed a job with the Neighborhood Playhouse. I worked with Aline Bernstein, the designer, painting scenery for the new season. While there, I met Remo Bufano, the puppeteer. He invited me to his studio and showed me his marionettes for *El Retablo de Maestro Pedro* by DeFalla. Bufano was an actor and, like me, a small–sized man.

Until that time, the thought of seriously entering the world of puppetry had not entered my mind. Here was an actor, an artist, who used puppets and marionettes for his creativity. I was intrigued by the possibility. I attended his performance of *Orlando Furioso* which was called "The Giant with the Enchanted Voice." The puppets were crudely made, small, but had the charm and individuality which characterize an artist. Bufano performed in a community center in Greenwich Village, and my expectations were not high. The curtain opened, revealing a simple stage with little scenery and no unusual lighting, but when the puppets began to move to his lines, I forgot they were puppets. They became alive and the giant really *did* have an enchanted voice. Bufano created an hypnotic illusion, a spell. He gave his puppets a dramatic power with so little theatrical effect I could not have conceived it had I not seen the performance. I carried away an impression that has never left me. I was now convinced that a dramatic reading had the power to transform the puppet into a human form with a magic that was pure theatre.

In 1927, when I returned to San Francisco with my new bride, Jo, I faced the problem of finding a direction for our lives. Like Alice in Wonderland, I was confused: ". . .which way . . . which way." I was still thinking about marionettes but uncertain where to begin. Jo and I rented an old house, and by some strange turn of fortune, in a vacant lot in back of this house, I found Blanding Sloan and Solomon, the weaver, who was living in another old house nearby. I felt I had come home again.

Blanding was living in a truck he had rigged up as studio/living quarters. We talked about marionettes and Bufano, and I dragged out my drawings of *Hamlet*. I told him about the wild idea I had of playing *Hamlet* with marionettes made from these drawings. "Why not?" he asked. Well, for one thing I didn't know how to begin; I had never made a marionette; I was not a craftsman and was not good with tools. "You see," I explained, "if I did it, they would have to be like my drawings."

"You can do it," he responded, in his usual encouraging manner. "All you need are wood, some scraps of leather, materials, glue, tacks, brads, a good jack knife, and you'll find a way."

Beryle Wynnyk, a young sculptor who lived next door, became very excited when we talked about a marionette *Hamlet*. She was then working with a puppeteer across from Washington Square, doing afternoon puppet shows for children. Fairy tales, I thought.

"You know, Vera's going to do Molierè's *The Doctor in Spite of Himself* with marionettes," Beryle said. Well, I thought, a classic with marionettes. "I'll be interested to see how it goes," I told her.

"She's looking for someone to play the doctor. Wouldn't you like to do it?" I said, "Yes."

Vera von Pillat had rented an old store near St. Mary's Church. She was small, dark, rather like a Gypsy, pleasant, but with a somewhat sharp tongue, and very positive in her ideas about puppets. Her place was very busy with several young women sewing for the puppets. Scraps of material were everywhere. Vera directed exactly how she wanted to dress the puppets. She was more accustomed to hand puppets than to marionettes. Her stringed figures were quite incredible. After trying one out, I was slightly skeptical as to what action I would be able to derive from them.

We began rehearsals of the Molière's play, in which I was playing Sgnarelle, the doctor. The marionettes were crudely made, small, very loosely jointed, and difficult to control. I found it impossible to make them walk properly. They were so light, it was hard to tell whether they were floating or actually had their two feet on the stage. As the legs wobbled at the knees, it made the characters weave back and forth when they should have been standing still. It was not what I expected of a classic marionette performance.

Opening night went much better than I had anticipated. There were laughs not entirely induced by the antics of the wobbly marionettes, proof that the audience was listening to the comedy lines of Molière's. The comedy itself held up even under such difficult circumstances. Because the play was short, Vera had added *The Sorcerer's Apprentice*, a version she had written for two marionettes built by Robert Howard. He was a very fine sculptor and had given the fully carved figures a somewhat Oriental character. In contrast to Vera's marionettes, Howard's were considerably larger. With careful lighting and a little magic mood music, it proved an interesting performance.

This experience did not discourage me from attempting my version of *Hamlet*. On the contrary, I found an opportunity to study what to correct when I built my marionettes. They would have to stand erect, move and posture gracefully, and above all, walk with dignity, the knees bending properly without moving in both directions.

At the time, the only book I could find with directions about how to build a marionette was one about Tony Sarg.* It contained diagrams and plans for building the body, the control, and where to attach the strings. The arms were cloth attached to the shoulders and tacked to a carved wooden forearm and hand. The shoulders and pelvis were cut out of wood and held together with cloth. The legs jointed at the knees were of wood with a cloth joint fastened to the pelvis. It looked very loose and flexible, suggesting the kind of body Vera had used. Although the basic idea was practical, I would have to develop a different structural pattern for the kind of marionette I would require for *Hamlet*.

*F.J. McIsaac, *The Tony Sarge Marionette Book,* B. W. Huebsch, New York, 1921.

THREE

Blanding brought me some scraps of sugar pine, soft and suitable for carving, and I found some pieces of redwood, not as good as the pine but light in weight. With a pocket knife and a few hand tools, I was ready to start my project.

I brought out my drawings for *Hamlet* and began carving. First, the heads. I made several heads, each time hoping to see Hamlet emerge from the piece of wood. As each head was completed, it seemed to take on a different character than that of Hamlet and was set aside to be cast as a possible Horatio, Laertes, or Bernardo. Each successive head seemed to come closer to the character. Soon I had carved all of the heads – all but Hamlet. I examined each head critically to see what I had missed. The tiny masks stared up at me, and I gave each one a part: this would be Horatio, this Claudius, this Polonius, this Laertes, and this wide–eyed, round childlike face would be Ophelia. I tried once more for Hamlet, and this time the narrow, gaunt, sensitive face of the melancholy Dane appeared, standing out in sharp contrast to the others, just as I had hoped.

The figures would have to be slender with small heads; the completed marionette measuring eighteen to twenty inches from head to toe and at least seven heads high. The proportions were extremely important if the characters were to appear tall. Unlike other marionettes I had seen, the heads were not to be more important than the rest of the body. I had carved the heads in simple planes to indicate facial and cranial structures with deep slits for the eyes. I had observed that puppet craftsmen usually concentrated on the head, working out the features in detail so that they would carry. My ideas differed.

After carving the heads, I began the bodies. I carved the legs, hands, and feet, then cut out wooden shoulders and hip pieces. The joint at the knees had to bend back not forward, so I devised a hinge joint with an insert of heavy leather glued into the slotted wood and fitted into a slot at the knee, pinned into place with an inch brad. I worked it back and forth and fitted it carefully until it moved freely. Then I weighted the carved feet with thin sheet lead and pinned them into the ankle slot. The lead weight was necessary to give the body proper balance, also so that you could feel the feet touch the floor.

11

They moved beautifully without sagging when held at the bridge rail level.

As each body was completed, I strung it to a simple airplane control and tested it – still looking for the graceful body I wanted for Hamlet. After many attempts I achieved one that worked. It didn't respond too well at first, but with a few adjustments and more manipulation practice, it began to move as I wanted.

The next step involved costuming the characters. I had painted the heads in neutral shades of greenish gray with blue or purple eye shadows, touches of a deeper shade to accentuate the planes, and bright carmine spots on the small mouths. Not until I had clothed the figures in simple costumes following my original designs did the characters come to life. I had used scraps of material from my wife Jo's collection. Hamlet was in dull black in contrast to the red of the King and the soft blue–green of the Queen's costume.

Hamlet's wig was simple: a light gray fringed material dusted with ocher. A plain white collar, silver chain and locket around his neck, and heavier chain around his waist were the only contrasting notes to the somber black tunic and tights.

The figure was so sensitive that the slightest movement of the control animated the marionette. With his feet firmly anchored to the floor, he could assume tragic attitudes by tilting the head or lifting the hand. With a subtle movement from side–to–side and a downward movement of the head, he breathed life into Shakespeare's soliloquies. By bringing the extended forefinger to his brow, he expressed deep thought. I saw my drawing coming alive. The rest of the experiment lay ahead.

In the process of building the marionettes, I became so absorbed in their construction that I gave no thought as to whether or not these characters would ever reach a marionette stage. I had only my studio in which to try them out. Just the making of them was a new experience.

Blanding visited the studio every day to watch my progress and always encouraged me.

"Keep it up," he said, "you're doing great."

Then one day he appeared and with a slight, casual drawl announced, "Get your cast together. We've got a theatre."

I was totally taken aback. As it turned out, he had rented a space behind a small lending library on Montgomery Street, where he planned to set up a large stage with curtains, lights, everything necessary to put on the show.

The reality he offered filled me with fear and challenged my boast of being capable of putting on a serious performance of *Hamlet* with marionettes. Who would I get to read the lines and manipulate?

Beryl Wynnyk was eager, and I cast her as Ophelia. She had a soft, plaintive voice, and I coached her in the part. Carol Beals, who had worked with Vera, was the right type for the Queen. Max McCarthy, a young Irishman with wild bushy hair, an habitue of Montgomery Street, and an aspiring actor with a deep voice, would make a good Claudius. I would play Hamlet, the Ghost, Polonius, the first Gravedigger, and other small parts if necessary. Two other recruits, Mervyn Leeds and Clarence Ferguson, would play Horatio and Laertes. Jo would handle the curtain, light changes, and the music. Mervyn would be in charge of the switchboard. That was the company. And we were going to make marionette history.

I called rehearsals, gave each his part, and instructed them to memorize their lines – the first order of business.

At first, the readings were not encouraging. No one in the company had played Shakespeare before. I worked very hard with each one, teaching the classic reading of blank verse. I wanted quality, a deep feeling for the characters, and, above all, Shakespeare's poetry had to be spoken with a lyrical rhythm. It was asking a lot from amateurs, but everyone cooperated, worked very hard, and was excited by the prospect. After several weeks, I felt encouraged by our efforts. We had undertaken a job that could result in a fiasco if the lines were not read with feeling and intensity. My whole theory about playing Shakespeare with marionettes depended on a convincing rendition of the text with my stringed figures serving as surrogates.

The next step was to manipulate the marionettes with the lines. That was the test and would only work if all of the lines had been memorized and well rehearsed before going on the bridge. But even after we had learned the lines, we found that when concentrating on manipulation, to make the actors walk and gesture properly, we forgot the lines and went blank. Stumbling and hard work, however, eventually made things fall into shape. The actors on the bridge lost themselves in their parts, coordinating the simple movements of the marionettes to the beauty of the speeches, and the play came to life.

Blanding had set up a large stage which gave the small marionettes unusual proportions. The stage consisted of two ten–foot bridges, a stage floor ten feet long and four–feet deep, with a proscenium height of nearly six feet. We were manipulating seven feet above the stage floor, which gave a feeling of tremendous depth from the front. From the back of the back bridge hung a sky drop that could be used as a shadow curtain when properly lighted. Blanding had rigged up seven ghost spots of three hundred and fifty watts each, focusing down from the front and sides. We used no floods or borders on stage, and each spot carried a different colored gelatin. This gave remarkable mobility to the faces and bodies, creating an illusion which was unbelievable when viewed from a short distance. The effect was magic – it held us under a spell, even from the bridge. This was a new theatre form (although as old in origin as theatre history) and not just another puppet show.

The marionettes were created in the greatest artistic simplicity, each revealing its individual character with hardly more than a suggestion of realism. The slim, blond Hamlet, dressed in black, stood in strong contrast to the pale, tragic Ophelia robed in a flowing pink silk gown. The evil Claudius was dressed in red; the palid Gertrude in blue–green; the youthful Laertes in a yellow tunic with black tights; the bald gray–bearded Polonius in blue–gray with a fur collar; the soldierly Horatio in steel–studded blue jerkin draped with a russet cloak; the two Guards: Bernardo and Marcellus, in rough burlap silvered to resemble chain mail; the two Gravediggers, the Priest, and the Pall Bearers in black, bearing the burial litter of Ophelia. This was our cast.

The costumes had been made from what material was available to me, and the settings were accomplished in the same manner. I had in my studio four rectangular wooden blocks, twenty–four inches by eight inches by four inches, which served as a basic unit set that could be arranged in various ways as levels for the marionettes to play upon.

The Queen's closet scene consisted of two muslin screens arranged at right angles forming four panels that framed an arched doorway. On the panels on each side of the arch, I painted the portraits of both Kings: Claudius and Hamlet's father. The sky drop shown at the back served as the shadow curtain for the King's ghost. To one side hung the arras behind which Polonius hides.

The spots were arranged to cover every playing area on the stage: three were fixed to the front bridge–rail, two on each side in the wings, and two on the floor in back of the sky curtain. We could also use special border lights on the floor under the back bridge. The back spots were used for projecting shadows such as the Ghost of Hamlet's father. The small switchboard that Mervyn had rigged up had three dimmers which controlled all the spots. With this simple arrangement, I could get any lighting effect I wanted.

As the figures were small and the distances they moved across not very large, our setup provided advantageous light for the marionettes, who were always brilliantly painted with colored lights, greatly enhancing the costume materials. The entire effect created the illusion of the marionettes as life size, a distinct advantage over the visual effect possible on a large stage.

When one sits in the balcony of an ordinary theatre, the actors always appear extremely distant. In contrast, the audience sitting twenty, thirty, or even fifty feet away from the marionette stage sees the whole picture in apparent life size. In films and on television, where every detail of an actor's face and expression is enlarged to fill a large screen, the viewer's imagination is robbed of its exercise. It is precisely the activation of the audience's imagination that is vital to the world of marionettes.

There were no microphones or public address systems in use when I gave my first performances. Tape recorders were unheard of, those delivering the lines from the marionette bridge had to project their voices and enunciate clearly in order to be heard and understood at the back of a small theatre. This provided the necessary intensity to the reading. Each performance was alive and spontaneous, an impossible occurrance when lines are taped beforehand. The performer and his audience came into direct contact.

Just as an actor performing on stage is stimulated by audience reaction, so were we stimulated while manipulating and delivering lines. It is the vibration sent out by the audience which is so important to puppeteers. We can feel it the moment the curtains part. It is that magic something that makes the theatre what it is.

This does not happen in a moving picture theatre or on a television screen. A film usually begins with background shots on which the credits are superimposed. Significant entrances for principal characters are nonexistent – entrances which in a stage performance are so carefully planned by the playwright, the director, and especially the actor if he knows his craft. The film actor's scenes are cut and edited to suit the director or editor. He has no control over what happens after his performance is completed; in many cases, his best efforts may land on the cutting–room floor. Nor does he benefit from audience reaction.

In comparison, how much more rewarding to the producer/actor/ director of a marionette show – he controls everything and is beholden to no one. It is this advantage which Gordon Craig considers in his book, *On the Art of the Theatre*, when praising the marionette as the ideal actor.

FOUR

To the pupils in my Dramatic College I put
the following question: "Do you consider
the Marionette natural?"
"No," they answered in one voice.
"What!" I replied indignantly. "Not
natural? All its movements speak with
perfect voice of its nature. If a machine
should try to move in imitation of human
beings, that would be unnatural. Now
follow me: the Marionette is more than
NATURAL; it has Style – that is to say,
UNITY OF EXPRESSION: therefore the
Marionette Theatre is the true theatre."

— Alexander Hevesi, Budapest

Edward Gordon Craig is the author of *On the Art of the Theatre*
and *Theatre Advancing*, two books which influenced me greatly before I went to New York in 1926. Two years later, when I began to
work on my first marionette production of *Hamlet*, I realized the
soundness of Craig's theories. He spoke of: ". . . puppets – marionettes – an Über–Marionette – a creature that could be controlled
by the artist."* It was a marvelous idea: to be able to make your own
actors, control their movements on stage, bring them to life with your
own voice, yourself unseen by the audience.

The Art of the Theatre is the same in one respect as any
other art. It is the work of one man – Unlike most other arts
it can only be seen and heard during the life of the man who
creates it – It cannot be copied for future generations by future Theatrical artists – It is necessary then, that it must be
accepted whilst this artist is still living. (Craig, *On the Art of
the Theatre*)

---

*E. Craig, *On the Art of the Theatre*.

17

As a young man, Gordon Craig was an actor with Sir Henry Irving's company. Ellen Terry, Craig's mother, was Irving's leading lady. Craig had directed his own company, travelling in the provinces of England, and had designed and directed experimental theatre. He influenced stage design and production here and in Europe and revolutionized the concept of theatre production during his lifetime. He was the theatre's chief revolutionary guiding spirit for more than fifty years.

Such was the vision I carried and which persuaded me to go ahead with a marionette production of *Hamlet*. Craig's own controversial production of *Hamlet* in Moscow in 1912 had aroused varied opinions and criticism. Somehow, it seemed logical that I should select *Hamlet* as my first play; in addition to which, I wanted to play the leading role myself.

> The actor must go, and in his place comes the inanimate figure – the Über–Marionette we may call him, until he has won for himself a better name. . . . today . . . many people come to regard him as a rather superior doll. This is incorrect. He is a descendant of the stone images of the old temples – he is today a rather degenerated form of a god.

> But as with all art which has passed into vulgar hands, the puppet has become a reproach. All puppets are now but low comedians. (Craig, *On the Art of the Theatre*)

Craig wrote a great deal more about all phases of modern theatre than he did about marionettes; nevertheless, he believed the marionette to be the "ideal actor."

He advised further: ". . . your aim is not to become a celebrated actor, it is not to become the manager of a so–called successful theatre; it is not to become the producer of elaborate theatre." I took his advice literally and put all the experience of my early apprenticeship in the theatre to use in becoming a puppeteer. I also became actor/manager/designer/producer, all rolled into one. Craig's advice was sound, and his theories, when put into practice, worked for me.

FIVE

There is only one actor – nay, one man – who has the soul of the dramatic poet and who has ever served as true and loyal interpreter of the poet. This is the Marionette. So let me introduce him to you.

— *Craig,* On the Art of the Theatre

I gave a lot of thought to what kind of puppet would best suit my purpose before starting to build my first show. I wanted the puppets to appear very tall, very graceful, and to move with dignity, yet easy flowing action that could be controlled by the puppeteer. Glove puppets, where the focus is on the head, were out of the question as they would not work as classic characters. Also, they are not operated on a stage; the puppeteers work standing with the puppets operated above their heads, which is very tiring on the arms and makes it impossible to actually view the figures in motion. I considered rod figures, but they, too, are controlled from below and only a limited depth of stage was providable with no practical stage floor, which would render them unsuitable. I then decided upon the stringed marionette. It could walk across the stage like a human, and the operator, looking down from a high bridge, could watch every movement as the strings were manipulated.

Working from two high bridges, the puppeteers would have adequate room to move about comfortably. In addition, the marionettes would not be restricted to lateral movements but could move freely in any direction so that compositions with the figures could be worked out with grouping, just as in a drawing. For me, it was the best medium with which to breathe life into the characters.

The construction of a marionette is no longer a mystery. Originally, puppeteers carefully guarded their secrets, fearing that special effects would be stolen from them by other puppeteers. Today, there are numerous books on marionettes, complete with diagrams, explanations of how to make different types of puppets and marionettes,

19

what materials to use, and how best to solve certain problems. The puppet craftsman must decide for himself what is best for him and invent his own method for solving his problem.

The artist creates a style. Usually, he achieves this by first making a drawing of his characters, then finding the materials which, when assembled, will bring this drawing to life. Sometimes this is done in collaboration with others who have special skills in costuming, carving, or painting. I believe the artist should do as much of the work himself as possible, for what emerges from the hand of the artist gives the marionette his individual style. The artist ceases his work when the marionette he is creating expresses his idea completely. He must always bear in mind that his marionette will be seen from a distance; finicky detail will only be superfluous.

A broad effect is preferable to a highly polished, overall finish. Texture is more important than a slick surface. This applies to both painted heads and hands. A swatch of strong color in a costume carries a greater distance than one made of rich brocade trimmed in braid and jewels. A carved head painted to look extremely realistic will appear inanimate on stage, whereas a head carved in simple planes, with the features strongly accented, will become surprisingly alive when properly lighted.

The artist must strive to achieve a quality of dramatic beauty, particularly in a classic production. This requires perfect coordination of all the elements of theatre. The beauty of costumes, the settings, the perfect craftsmanship of the carvings – all must work together to provide the essential total effect. Only then does the audience experience that spell which remains in memory long after the completion of the play.

All these factors impressed me greatly when reading Gordon Craig's book, but not until I had tested them myself in my first show, did I realize how right he was.

He had been right, too, in selecting *Hamlet* for his great experiment at the Moscow Art Theatre. Knowing that the selection of the play is all important, I also felt right in choosing it as my first experiment with marionettes. It was a tremendous challenge, and I wanted the results to be equally provocative.

SIX

Never copy the old but never forget the old, for there is always some good to be found in it.

— *Craig,* Theatre Advancing

The selection of a play or the material for it is always the puppet producer's first problem. Not every play is suitable. As the marionette is basically a theatrical form, careful consideration must be given to what it is best capable of performing. It has been most successful in comedy and fantasy but it is seldom, if ever or hardly ever, used to play tragedy. The reason is obvious. Hand puppets are a natural medium for characters who express grotesque and comic personalities. Their large heads and broad movements immediately induce laughter. They are equally effective in fantasies portraying half–human, half–animal legendary characters, such as demons or others who permit the artist to allow his imagination to run riot. In this category, they are more believable than humans. So, puppeteers have remained dedicated to legend, folklore, and comedy, which are never questioned when played by puppets. As an instrument of theatre, the potential of the puppet and the marionette has not been explored.

Regardless of whether or not he decided to play in any of these categories, it must be emphasized that the artist/actor/puppeteer must select play material best suited to his own talents, taking into consideration the limitations of the marionettes.

To me there is ever something more seemly in man when he invents an instrument and through that instrument translates his message. (*Craig,* On the Art of the Theatre)

Above all, one must avoid the naturalistic. A modern, contemporary play depending on realistic situations and characters is not a good selection. The results would be dull. The artist/puppeteer must, therefore, choose something that will fire his imagination in order to give an exciting performance to which his audience will react in a like manner.

21

Basic theatrical elements, dramatic quality and brilliant lines abound in Shakespeare's plays, and there are many to choose from for the puppeteer. Pure theatre and sophisticated period comedy exist in Molière's plays. Many of his comedies could have been written for puppets, as many of his characters have been taken out of the *commedia dell'arte*. These plays require good actors, and I firmly believe a good puppeteer should be a good actor. Good manipulation comes with rehearsal and practice, but it is no substitute for poor reading. A good actor can be trained to be a good manipulator, but a poor actor will never make his marionette convincing no matter how well he manipulates. Therefore, in selecting a play for marionettes, the producer should always look for characters and situations that will provide exercise for the actor/puppeteer's talents.

I carefully considered all the visual and theatrical possibilities before deciding to attempt *Hamlet* with marionettes. I selected scenes that had dramatic impact and could be staged effectively on the marionette stage. They necessitated visual as well as dramatic interest.

When the curtain opened on the throne room, all the central characters were on stage. The relationship between Hamlet, his uncle, now the King, and his mother, the Queen, were immediately established. Hamlet's suspicion of his uncle, his revulsion of his mother, so soon married after his father's death, were quickly revealed. Following this, Horatio entered, announcing to Hamlet that his father's Ghost had appeared to him on the platform while he, Bernardo, and Marcellus were on watch. All of this, in one short scene, provided the whole plot of the play and a gripping suspense at the curtain. The next scene followed with the appearance of the Ghost. Real excitement existed, and it gave the marionettes every opportunity to hold the audience in its spell.

Then came the entrance of Polonius, the old minister (serio–comic), exclaiming Hamlet's madness to the King and Queen, which led into Hamlet's scene with Polonius; the entrance of the players; and the soliloquy: "Now I am alone . . ." followed by the scene between Ophelia and Hamlet. I included the play within the play: the King's repentance scene; the Queen's closet scene; the Gravediggers' scene with its comedy relief; the burial of Ophelia; and concluded with the duel between Hamlet and Laertes. In spite of the shortened version of the play, the story was complete and the beauty of Shakespeare's lines carried just as they would have on a large stage. The audience was greatly moved, which proved to me that my selection had been right.

My next problem was to follow *Hamlet* with an equally dramatic and forceful production.

SEVEN

Drama is a natural consequence of fine theatre.

— *Craig,* Theatre Advancing

In New York in 1926, I saw Charles Gilpin play Eugene O'Neill's *The Emperor Jones*. The play had impressed me with its exciting dramatic climaxes that built gradually toward a powerfully suspenseful finale. I read the play, considered its exciting visual and dramatic possibilities, and decided upon it as my next marionette production. This would prove an entirely new challenge. The character of Brutus Jones is the antithesis of Hamlet. The play was contemporary, affording me the opportunity to test the potential of the marionette in a different category.

The play is short, dramatic with few characters, and two sure–fire theatrical gimmicks: a gunshot at the end of every forest scene and a tom–tom thumping to represent an increasing heart–beat throughout the entire performance, increasing the suspense to the very climax of the play.

The script requires good acting, good timing, and an understanding of the character's psychology. Brutus Jones is an ex–Pullman porter who, after killing a guard, escapes from a chain gang in the South. He finds his way to a remote, uncharted island in the West Indies and, with sheer bravado, makes himself emperor. The opening scene is a stark throne room with a suggestion of the jungle seen through a doorway at the back. An old native woman is seen escaping and is stopped by a Cockney trader, Smithers. The natives are in revolt and have fled the palace. As the native woman leaves, Jones enters and is confronted by Smithers, who informs him of the revolt. The Emperor brags that he has no fear of an uprising but has planned an escape in the event of such a happening.

He starts on his escape trek through the forest, intending to make his way to the coast where he hopes to find a boat to take him safely to Martinique. As he begins his journey, the native tom–toms start beating in synchronization with his heart. He has six bullets in his gun, one of silver which he plans to use on himself if necessary. There are six forest scenes; at the end of each, Jones fires his gun at an apparition. His fear mounts as he fails to find his previously stored caches of food. Stumbling through the forest, he becomes more confused and frightened as the apparitions carry him back into his past. Exhausted, he discards his boots and coat, kneels down in his tattered uniform and prays. A witch doctor appears, performing a wild voodoo dance; a crocodile emerges from out of the river. In his fear, Jones panics and shoots the crocodile. He has completely circled the island, coming back to the edge of the woods, where the natives await him. At their chief's signal, the natives start shooting. The cracks of their rifles are heard. A moment of suspense ensues before Jones is brought in dead. Smithers stares at him and exclaims: "Gawd blimey! Silver bullets – but ye died in the 'eighth of style, anyhow."

The settings were designed by Blanding Sloan, as were the shadow figures used for the apparitions. They were cut–outs with a single movement controlled by a string. They appeared when colored lights were projected on them from the back. By arranging the lights in different positions, the shadows became superimposed, one upon the other, producing an abstract effect. As Jones goes deeper into the forest, the apparitions become more abstract. The tom–tom beats faster and faster until the gunshot. The apparitions disappear as Jones fires at them. The tom–tom rhythm slows as the curtain closes, not ceasing until the final gunshot. Each scene builds in intensity. The audience could be heard counting the shots as the scenes progressed.

The trees were made of black felt cut–outs and twisted materials, giving the effect of gnarled tree trunks. By rearranging the trees, which were hung on a track, and moving the rocks around on the stage, each scene change was easily achieved. By bunching the trees and rocks closer together as the scenes progressed, we were able to create a feeling of density.

The character of Jones required giving a feeling of strength and power to a small figure less than twenty inches tall. The negro dialect came easily for me, but the strength and power had to come with the voice. I pitched my voice two octaves lower, and when Jones came on, resplendent in his gaudy red and blue uniform trimmed in gold braid, something extraordinary happened: the small figure became the brutal, boasting Pullman porter turned emperor.

Just recently, I met Kermit Love, the puppeteer responsible for the large monsters on the Muppet Show. He told me he had seen my original performance of *Emperor Jones* in 1928 and said he came away with the impression that the puppeteer playing Jones must have been a man of gigantic strength and power. Jones was only eighteen inches tall, and I am five feet, four inches tall. I mention this to illustrate the power of the human voice and its life-giving power when animating a marionette.

On opening night, the audience left spellbound. All the newspapers reviewed the performance, and we had another hit show. By now, I was fully convinced the human voice had the power to bring to life the dramatic instrument we call the marionette – an unbeatable combination when the marionette is subtly and carefully controlled by the actor/puppeteer. Few puppeteers have taken full advantage of this or developed their voices to the point of being able to do so. If I could perform successfully two such diverse plays as *Hamlet* and *The Emperor Jones*, I would be able to go on with other plays.

As a prologue to *Emperor Jones*, I read portions of Vachael Lindsay's *Congo* to the beating of a tom-tom with a solitary voodoo figure seated center stage. This mysterious witch doctor moved to the rhythm of his own beating of a tom-tom, bathed in a blood-red light from one side and an acid-green light from the other. As an opening, it set the mood perfectly.

The first two plays had been both dramatically and visually exciting. They necessitated the dramatic movement so essential to a successful marionette production. While the voices were life-size to bring the figures to life-size, the movements of the figures were kept in proportion to their small size. Over-manipulation can prove a fault in this kind of play. The success of these factors contributed to the positive reception of *The Emperor Jones* as a marionette play. I would not forget them in my future productions. I was excited by the selection of my next play.

EIGHT

It is the particular power which belongs to man alone and to him through his intelligence and his will that makes the artist.

— *Craig,* On the Art of the Theatre

It was Shakespeare's *Macbeth* which I chose to follow *The Emperor Jones*. It had all of the qualities of my two previous plays and provided the actor/puppeteer with a great dramatic part. Witches, ghosts, murders, all set in early tribal Scotland, join the central character's vaulting ambition that determines his fateful end. *Macbeth* also provided a field day for the designer.

The settings called for rugged, craggy forms, the bleak rocky moor, and a cave setting of supernatural eerieness for the apparitions of the ghosts. The designer would have complete architectural freedom to use semi–abstract shapes to create the feeling of impending doom.

By now, I was learning how to build the kind of instrument that would respond to my reading of Shakespeare's lines. I was developing confidence in the medium. I had to conceive new characters in a different mood – different from the other two plays.

This was a challenge to test the ability of the marionette to be convincing in an entirely different tone. The stage pictures would be as important as theatre. The Scots were rough, barbaric tribesmen, and to create that effect, I began with rough black and white charcoal drawings of the characters from which I would build my marionettes. The drawings had exactly the texture I wanted. The problem was to bring them to life.

I realized I would first have to costume the figures in white, then texture them with black paint and a dry brush to make them look like the charcoal sketches. After building the figures, I dressed them in thin unbleached muslin, draped them, tacked and sewed the material in place, carrying out the lines of my drawings. After I gave them the texture with the dry brush, they began to resemble the characters I had drawn on paper, but they still needed some color. I then mixed aniline dyes in various colors, and with a brush, applied the colors directly on the costumed marionettes. My tribesmen looked like water color sketches. After completion, I hurriedly strung them, hung them on stage, and turned on a flood of various colored lights. The effect was magic. Macbeth and the other characters were just like my drawings but in three dimension.

The Witches, dressed in filmy dark gauze streaked with color, flew in and out of the sky like large bats, accompanied by the sound of thunder. A white light moving across the sky in forked steaks gave the needed effect of lightning. The heath was represented by an almost bare stage with cut–out rocks draped in dark cloth silhouetted against the sky. A rise of ground front and left appeared where Macbeth and Banquo make their first appearances.

I opened with the Witches' scene, Act I, Scene 1, combined with Act I, Scene 3, the entrance of Macbeth and Banquo, thus eliminating the second scene with Duncan.

The Witches were flown in from above and huddled together in silhouette against a menacing sky that moved from a strong blue–green to a deep purple. No better scene for a marionette has been written. I cut the play to move swiftly and with dramatic impact – from the Witches' opening to the final duel between Macbeth and MacDuff.

Lady Macbeth enters reading the letter from Macbeth, followed by his entrance, and her plot to murder Duncan. After his arrival, Duncan exits with his sons to be housed for the night. Macbeth, finding himself alone, addresses his soliloquy to the bloody red dagger that appears on the low wall at back with lighting and is dimmed out as Macbeth exits to commit the murder. The comedy scene, provided by the Porter's entrance as MacDuff and Lennox knock loudly at the gate, breaks the tension, but the suspense is heightened and builds to a climax after they discover the murder of Duncan, and: "Most sacriligious murder hath broke ope – the Lord's annointed temple . . . ." Our marionettes held the attention of the audience in this scene as effectively as when it is played by human actors.

The other scenes played equally well: the instructions to kill Banquo; the banquet scene with the appearance of Banquo's bloody ghost; the Witches' cave scene, conjuring up before Macbeth the apparitions of dead kings, predicting his eventual doom.

As I recited the lines and looked down on the small wooden actors below, they became more real to me than any living actors. I was moved and, as with *Hamlet*, felt much like an orchestra conductor directing a great symphony as I timed the action and reading of the lines by the company on the bridge. *Macbeth* had proved a good choice. I knew now that the marionettes could play poetic tragedy and melodrama as well as comedy.

I must emphasize once more that it is not the marionette, the costume, the settings, the lighting alone that create the magic. Above all, the power is in the voice of the actor and the feeling he is able to express through his instrument. This combined with the implements of the theatre add up to a compelling performance. When everything works together, and only then, do the actors and the audience become totally involved in what is being seen and heard.

When the solo puppeteer, the skilled manipulator, performs with his marionette, he is an entertainer. He has rehearsed and performs his act to a point of perfection. He intrigues his viewers with his subtlety of manipulation. The focus is on clever manipulation.

The dramatic actor/puppeteer differs. His talent lies in his power to use his voice with which he hypnotizes his listeners. When this talent is used in a dramatic play with marionettes, it can hold an audience even though the actor is an eighteen–inch jointed, wooden figure controlled by strings. If this were not possible, then *Macbeth* would not have been possible with marionettes.

An extremely important ingredient I used in painting a stage picture was color. I used colored lighting as I would use paint on a canvas. Instead of lighting up the whole stage, I concentrated the lighting on the areas where figures were moving, increasing or decreasing the lighting for contrast. I used strong reds and blues from either side, accentuated with pinks, greens, and purples, and an occasional highlighting of straw or amber. I never used white lights. If anyone complained of being unable to see the faces, I told them that the scene was more important than the faces. As so often happened with this kind of marionette play, what the audience did not see, they imagined, and when this happened, as it often did, I knew I had achieved my purpose.

During this time, I was very fortunate to find many willing volunteers to work in the shows. Any young aspirant to puppetry who was willing to donate either his time back stage or on the bridge was immediately put to work. If someone had no experience, I trained him/her in reading and manipulation. I had three young sisters, newly arrived from New Orleans, who became very excited by my project and insisted on becoming a part of it. They seemed to have a natural inclination for the theatre. Each was a totally different type: Yvonne was twenty–two and rather shy. With hard work, she played some of the women's roles. Leslie, nineteen, was a throw back to our Irish ancestry and had more spirit. She proved to be an excellent Lady Macbeth. Ding (Marcelle) was lively, with a good sense of humor, and played comedy roles. This was in the tradition of puppetry wherein entire families participated in puppet shows. With the help of my sisters and others, I had a fairly well–balanced company, full of youthful enthusiasm that provided me with the incentive to attempt many plays that other puppeteers would not have considered puppet material.

Jo, my wife, was a wonderful partner in my venture. Being of a more practical nature than the rest of us, she took over the box office and distribution of the hand–printed block posters I designed for the various shows, all of which were printed on an old–fashioned hand–laundry wringer. The prints later became collectors' items. We received a great deal of news coverage. The marionette theatre had become a San Francisco institution.

NINE

All the world's a stage
And all the men and women merely players.

— Shakespeare, *As You Like It*

After completing the run of *Macbeth* in Blanding Sloan's theatre, I decided to open a theatre of my own. I found an empty wine cellar on the ground floor of the old Montgomery Block building. The rent was right, fifty dollars a month, and it was near 718 Montgomery. The cellar was on Merchant Street, in an alley occupied by a wholesale meat market. Next door to us was a speakeasy and in the middle of the block, a fish market. Despite this rather unfavorable location, the cellar provided plenty of space for both my theatre and workshop. Actually, when the wind wasn't blowing in our direction, the place was ideal. Thus was formed The Marionette Guild.

As the three plays I had produced at 718 Montgomery were tragedies, I decided to do a comedy. Puppets had always been popular in broad comedy, Punch and Judy, even satirical buffoonery, but a classic comedy with marionettes would be different, presenting me with another new challenge.

My father had always been a devoted reader of Molière and would read to us children in French: scenes from *Don Juan*, *L'Avare*, *Le Bourgeois Gentilhomme*, and his other favorites. I immediately thought of *Don Juan*. It had the same basic elements of great theatre found in Shakespeare and O'Neill, in addition to being a great satirical comedy. It was visually perfect, possessing the supernatural quality that mystifies audiences. It would afford me the opportunity to design settings and costumes for a period different than that of the other plays we had produced.

The play is exciting in the contrast of the two great characters: Don Juan, the arrogant, conceited, elegant seducer; Sganarelle, Don Juan's servant – meek, faithful, appalled by his master's transgressions.

31

Although the play is in five acts, I made many cuts as a number of scenes are unnecessary in furthering the story. I eliminated Act II, which deals with the peasants, shortened others, reduced the characters to nine, told the story in five scenes, and performed it with four different settings. As the period is 17th Century, I dressed Don Juan in the style of a cavalier.

The characters were not difficult to cast and my company, those who had worked with me in other shows, easily handled the parts. The characters of Don Juan and Sganarelle presented some difficulties as these two are on stage the entire time. I chose to play Sganarelle, the role originally played by Molière, but finding someone to play the difficult part of Don Juan, as I wanted it read, presented a problem. I tried out several male voices but none possessed the dash, the arrogance, or the contrast necessary in playing opposite Sganarelle. The exchange had to be rapid, the long speeches carefully timed, and delivered with vigor and authority or the scenes would die. Unsuccessful in finding the right Don Juan, I decided to play both parts myself. I used two distinct voice levels: Don Juan's contrasted sharply to the timid, high-pitched Sganarelle. I delivered Don Juan's lines at a faster pace than those of Sganarelle. The exchange of comedy dialogue I carried off at a lively pace. No one suspected that the voices of the swash-buckling master and the ridiculous little servant were read by the same person. Eventually, the two characters came through as I wished.

The brilliant, satirical humor in Molière's lines provided excellent material for the marionettes. Sganarelle constantly reproaches his master for his dissolute life. The suspenseful moment in the forest when they discover the statue of the commander whom Don Juan has killed begins as a comic scene, and when Don Juan taunts the statue, inviting him to dinner, Sganarelle laughingly goes along with the joke. When, however, the statue nods his head in acceptance, Sganarelle, in fear, falls trembling to the ground. He and his master flee as the curtain falls.

The marionette statue comes to life and appears in Don Juan's dining room. Terrified, Sganarelle hides behind his master. It is a scene that might have been written for marionettes, as is the last act which takes place in the forest before the statue. Don Juan's father appears, begging his son to repent his ways. Don Juan promises to do so, and when the father departs, Sganarelle expresses his joy on hearing of his master's change of heart. Don Juan laughs and delivers his long speech on hypocrisy. In tears, Sganarelle reveals his horror and delivers his very confused comic speech.

The time of reckoning arrives. In thunder and lightning, the statue again comes to life. He extends his hand and beckons Don Juan to follow. Defiantly, Don Juan takes the statue's hand. The earth opens with flashes of red fire and smoke. Flying devils from

Hell howl around Don Juan. He is consumed, dragged into the flames by the devils, while Sganarelle is left, kneeling, trembling in fear. As he leaves the stage in tears, he cries out: "My wages . . . my wages . . . my wages." The curtain falls. It is a scene no audience can resist. It never failed to bring down the house.

Here again, the union of comedy, tragedy, and the supernatural provided brilliant material for the marionette. Molière's prose gives the actor/puppeteer all he needs to bring forth an inspired performance. Although I have played Sganarelle on stage, the thrill of bringing both characters to life with marionettes of my own creation far surpassed that experience. I had much more control and was able to present my own interpretation of both characters.

Here is an example of the dramatic advantage the marionette has over the live stage actor. The scenic effects were visually exciting and very easily achieved. As the base for the unit set, I used two large, empty cardboard columns bought at a display supply house. I added balcony pieces against a sky drop with a row of shadowy trees on a track under the back bridge. The addition of heavy drapes and furniture created the dining room. When removed, I had the palace exterior. By adding more trees to cover the columns, the forest scene for the statue was effected. It appears on cue with lighting changes. The result was more effective than it would have been on a large stage.

By using the high double bridges, puppeteers can exchange marionettes by merely handing them across to one another when crosses are necessary. The chief puppeteer can remain on his own side, manipulating another character, while the one he has just handled is exited by the operator opposite him. When I was talking for Don Juan, someone else held Sganarelle. I would retrieve him when speaking his lines. In this manner, the character I was voicing was always in my hands, and I could thus control the movements of both characters.

Don Juan was always popular with my audiences and made an excellent addition to my repertoire. Like Shakespeare, Molière wrote his plays as they were being rehearsed, making corrections as he went along. And like Shakespeare, Molière was an actor, in this case, the principal actor in his own company.

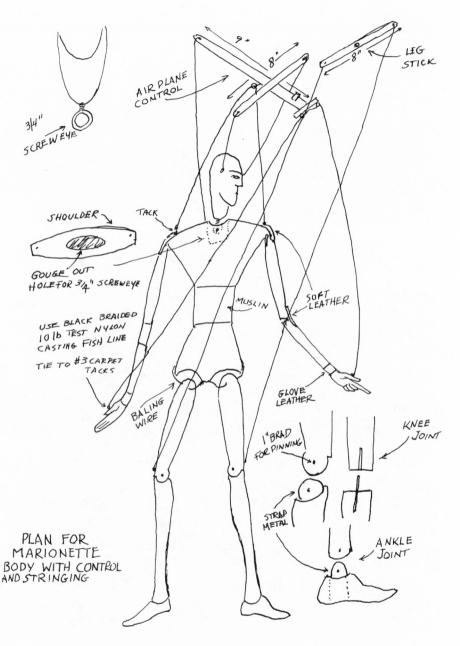

3/4"
SCREW EYE

AIRPLANE
CONTROL

9"

8"

8"

LEG
STICK

SHOULDER

TACK

GOUGE OUT
HOLE FOR 3/4" SCREWEYE

MUSLIN

SOFT
LEATHER

USE BLACK BRAIDED
10 lb TEST NYLON
CASTING FISH LINE

TIE TO #3 CARPET
TACKS

BALING
WIRE

GLOVE
LEATHER

1" BRAD
FOR PINNING

KNEE
JOINT

STRAP
METAL

ANKLE
JOINT

PLAN FOR
MARIONETTE
BODY WITH CONTROL
AND STRINGING

Drawing of the basic structural form used for all of Chessé's
marionettes.

Hamlet, 1928. Photo by Chessé.

Ralph Chessé with the cast of *Hamlet*, 1928.

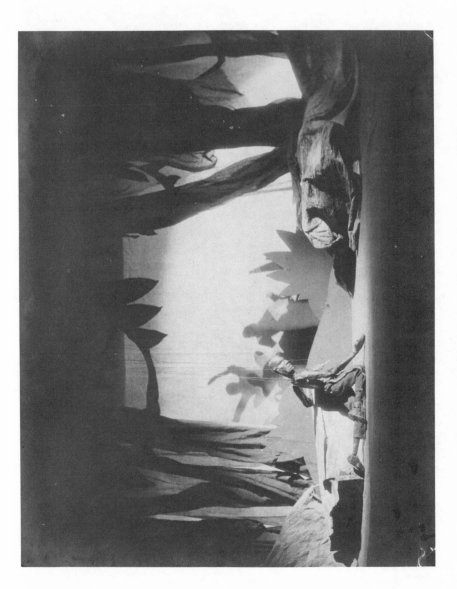

Jones and the Galley Slaves, *The Emperor Jones*, 1928.

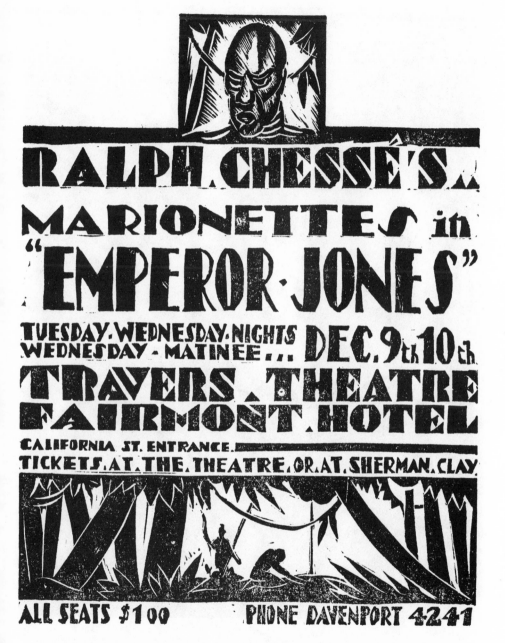

Poster by Ralph Chessé. Eugene O'Neill's *The Emperor Jones*, 1929 production. Linoleum blockprint.

Lady Macbeth and Macbeth, 1928. Photo by William Horace Smith.

Don Juan and Sganarelle, his servant, Molière's *Don Juan*, 1929.

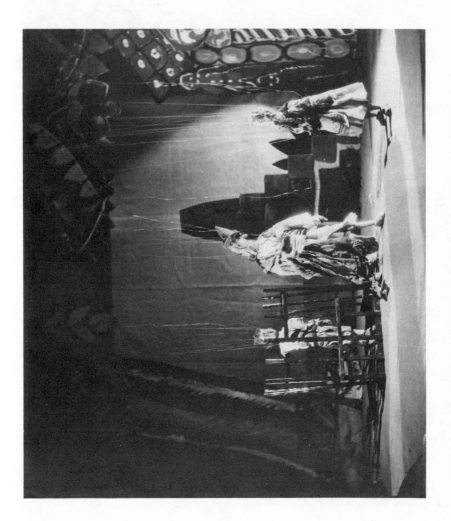

Hansel, The Witch, Gretel, from *Hansel and Gretel*, 1930. Photo by Dorothy Moore.

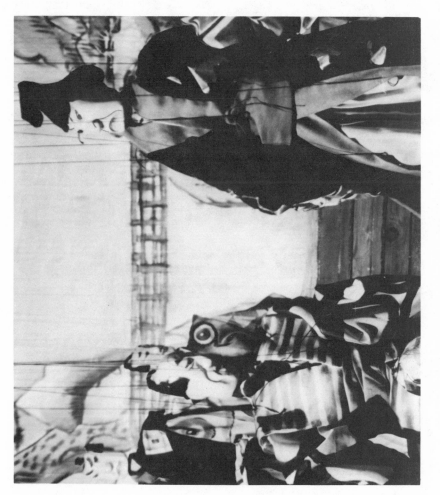

Pooh Bah, Koko, Pish Tush, The Mikado, from Gilbert and Sullivan's *The Mikado*, 1930 production.

"SIEGFRIED"

with RALPH-CHESSÉ'S MARIONETTES

THURS. FRI. SAT.
OCT. 1-6-7-8-13-14-15
at 8:30 P. M.

SATURDAY MATINEES
OCT. 1-8-15 at 2:30 P. M.

FOR
RESERVATIONS
PHONE ORDWAY 3994

TICKETS 50 CENTS

MARIONETTE GUILD ᴧᴧᴧᴧ

718 MONTGOMERY ST.
SAN FRANCISCO . . .

Poster for *Siegfried*, 1932. Linoleum print by Chessé.

The Shepherds and Angel Gabriel, *Noel*, by Maurice Bouchor, 1932.

The Marionette Guild — 1932-34.
1749 CLAY ST.

Drawing of the 1749 Clay Street Theatre, 1932–34.

HAMLET

RALPH CHESSE'S MARIONETTES every **FRIDAY** and **SATURDAY** at 8:30 PM in **JANUARY**

MARIONETTE GUILD .... 1749 CLAY ST. ORDWAY 3041. 3994

TICKETS 55 cents

ON SALE AT CITY of PARIS

Poster for *Hamlet*, 1932 revival. Linoleum print.

Queen and King of Hearts, White Rabbit, Alice, from *Alice in Wonderland*, 1934. Photo by Lauzun.

Alice, Tweedledee, Tweedledum, from *Alice in Wonderland*, 1934.
Photo by Lauzun.

THE MISER

French Comedy by Molière

WITH

RALPH CHESSE'S MARIONETTES

MARIONETTE-GUILD, 718 *Montgomery Street*

THURS., FRI., SAT. NIGHTS

NOV. 3-4-5-10-11-12 at **8:30 P. M.**

For Reservations Phone
ORdway 3994   *Tickets 50 Cents*

Poster for *The Miser*, 1930. Linoleum cut by Chessé.

The Tinkers, Woman of the Road, Philosopher, from *The Crock of Gold*. 1936. Federal Theatre Project, San Francisco.

Jones and the Crocodile, *The Emperor Jones*, 1937. Los Angeles Marionette Project. Ralph Chessé, Director.

The Witch and Snow White, *Snow White and the Seven Dwarfs*, 1939. Federal Theatre Project, Treasure Island World's Fair.

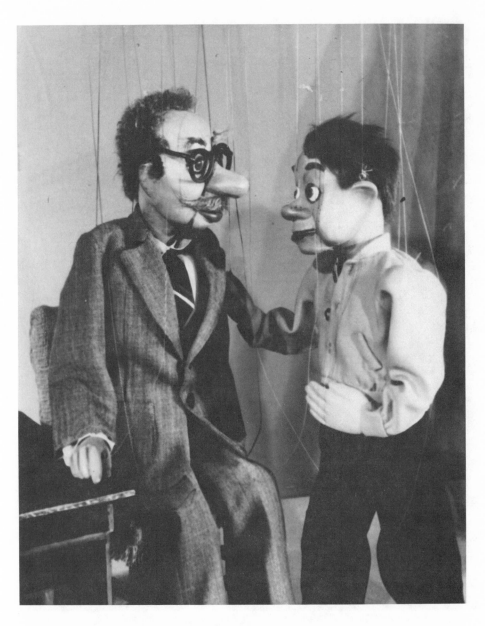

Baron Woodley and Willie, from the television program, *Willie and the Baron*, created by Ralph Chessé for KGO(ABC), 1951.

Sherlock Holmes and Dr. Watson, from
Willie and the Baron, 1951.

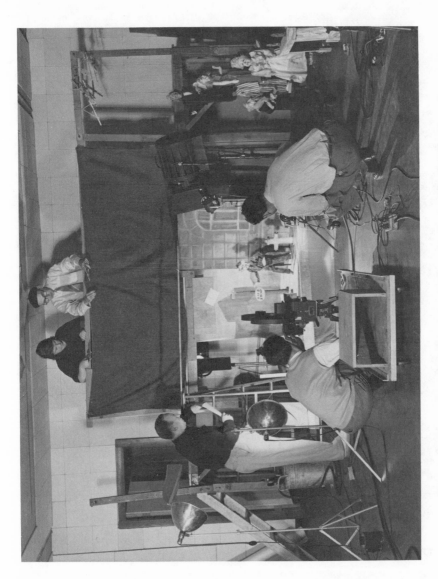

Filming the Calso commercials, Lettie Connell and Ralph Chessé on the bridge, 1951.

Calso and the Man with Indigestion, 1951.

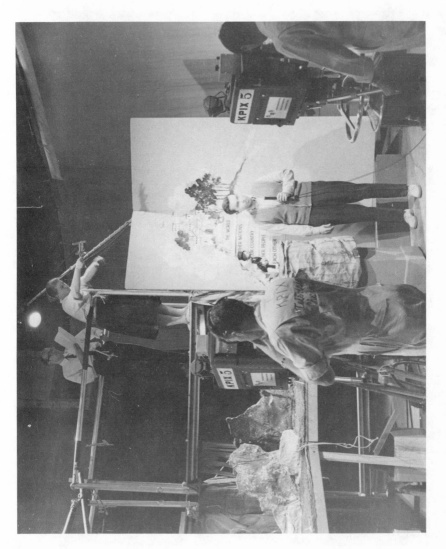

Filming *Brother Buzz*, on the bridge, Dion Chessé and Lettie Connell, 1954.

Brother Buzz and Miss Busy Bee, leading characters from *The Brother Buzz Show*, 1952–66.

Flittermouse the Bat, from *The Brother Buzz Show*.

Stumpy Swift the Lizard and Buzz, from *The Brother Buzz Show*.

Macbeth and Lady Macbeth. The 1979 production of *Macbeth*.

Chessé's final Shakespearean production. Scenes from the production. Photos by Hal Gibson, taken during performance.

1972 portrait of Ralph Chessé by Margo Moore.

TEN

Avoid the so-called "naturalistic" in movement as well as in
scenes and costume.

— Craig, On the Art of the Theatre

I now felt it time to balance my repertoire with a play that would
appeal to children but also hold the interest of an adult audience.
There were always the Saturday matinees to which parents brought
their children. This time the young audience could bring their parents. My choice was an adaptation of the opera *Hansel and Gretel* by
Humperdinck.

As I had contacts with a voice teacher and a group of young
singers, I arranged to have them sing the principal arias and choruses.
I sang the Father's principal solo, and using the libretto for the spoken lines, I played the Witch in recitative, singing only her ·dance
number, which produced a more dramatic effect. Excellent recordings were available which I used for overtures and background.

Using the libretto and presenting *Hansel and Gretel* as part op-
era/part play made it acceptable to audiences of all ages. I preferred
it as a marionette play rather than as grand opera. The fantasy was
more believable with marionettes than with humans. The theatrical
gimmicks – the explosion of the oven, the burning of the Witch, and
the finale when the gingerbread children come to life – provided excellent puppet material. The illusion was complete. The characters
were brought to life by the artist's imagination.

When selecting their plays, puppet showmen, like others in
"show business," usually think in terms of audience appeal and box
office attraction. I decided to avoid that trap as it would restrict me
from doing what I really wanted. When I did compromise and selected a play that had appeal for young audiences, I selected it,
firstly, because it appealed to me and hoped it would be of interest to
other adults. I thereby avoided the favorite nursery tales that most
puppeteers find easy to sell. My theory proved sound and always
worked for me.

35

Over a period of years, I adapted *The Moor's Legacy* from Washington Irving's stories of the Alhambra, *The Tinderbox* by Hans Christian Andersen, *The Chinese Nightingale*, as well as an adult version of *Alice in Wonderland*. The Lewis Carroll story was combined with *Through the Looking Glass* inspired by the script used by Eva LeGallienne in New York. Once again, these productions appealed to theatre goers of all ages.

Many puppeteers possess the gift of being able to communicate directly with children through the medium of puppetry. The children talk with the puppets. When this happens, the children become a vital part of the performance. I have always enjoyed being part of this kind of audience. In my own work, however, I was seldom able to achieve this. Each puppeteer must find the medium best suited to his particular talent. I developed my own kind of theatre, one in which drama and comedy would be presented strictly as theatre form. It was this theatricality of puppetry that appealed to me.

On one occasion, I adapted an old Gothic folk tale written for puppets by Professor Mathurin Dondo, who at the time was teaching French at the University of California, Berkeley. He used it in his French classes and gave me permission to adapt it for the marionette stage. He called it *The Pie and the Tart*. It involves two clever beggars who scheme to get a free meal of a pie and tart they see in the baker's window, but the pie and tart had been ordered for a party given by the town mayor.

On the same program, I adapted *The Man Who Married A Dumb Wife*, an old folk tale written by Anatole France and originally produced as a stage play by Granville Barker. I had played in the stage version in New Orleans and recognized its possibilities as a marionette play. At that time, I had made up the actors in an exaggerated manner resembling puppets, using large noses and grotesque features built up with nose putty. The story involves an old French judge married to a very beautiful young girl who is unable to speak. Three famous local doctors are reported to possess the power of restoring her speech. The judge calls them in; they perform the operation; she regains her ability to speak but talks incessantly. In desperation, the judge again summons the doctors, begging them to make his wife dumb again. This they cannot do. They can only make the judge deaf. To this, he assents.

These two short plays provided excellent material for both adults and children. They contained all the theatrical qualities for which I searched.

While on Merchant Street, Jack Ford, a young puppet enthusiast with an original feeling for character, had given matinees in Blanding Sloan's theatre. Jack wanted to perform Gilbert and Sullivan's *Iolanthe* with marionettes. I thought it an interesting idea and was curious to see how it would work. Jack was a teenager, a college student, and an excellent performer with a great sense of humor. He had a unique way of performing his handpuppet shows, improvising the dialogue as he went along, feeding the lines to whomever he could get to assist him. He couldn't do that with Gilbert and Sullivan, but with the music played by a pianist, he sang the three principal roles: the Lord Chancellor, the Fairy Queen, and Sergeant Willis. Some of the singers who had played in *Hansel and Gretel* filled out the rest of the cast.

His small marionettes had great character but were very loosely put together. In some cases, the strings were attached with pins. Sometimes a string would come loose, but Jack was undaunted and always managed to give a great performance. It was a delightful experience and started me thinking about what other Gilbert and Sullivan operas I might be able to do. As some of them were recorded by d'Oyly Carte Opera Company, it occurred to me they might be used by filling in the dialogue with our puppeteers.

While we were on Merchant Street, Sir Phillip Ben Greet came to town with his Shakespearean company, giving performances of the First Quarto version of *Hamlet*. Ben Greet was an old trouping Shakespearean who, along with Sir Frank Benson, had done much to keep the Shakespearean spirit alive with his touring company. Louis Stellman, a columnist on *The San Francisco Call-Bulletin*, suggested I invite Ben Greet to the theatre and perform some scenes with my marionettes. I was delighted by the opportunity. Stellman made the arrangements, and Sir Phillip arrived with some of the members of his company. He was a large, pleasant man sporting a thick mane of grey hair. We did the Gravediggers' scene from *Hamlet*, and the Witches' scene from *Macbeth*. These noted actors came to be amused but were completely absorbed by what they saw.

"Splendid," said Sir Phillip after the show. "This was better than what I have seen at the Royal Theatre in London." He seemed sincere in his praise and later wrote me a letter of congratulations which included an autographed picture. Flattered, I hoped what he had said was true.

The old Montgomery Block building which housed The Marionette Guild was almost entirely tenented by the artists, poets, and writers of San Francisco's bohemia. It seemed the most logical place for a marionette theatre. It also proved to be the breeding ground for the rats that raided the garbage cans kept in a closet just upstairs above the theatre. Often, during a dramatic soliloquy, we heard scampering and loud screeching noises emanating from the rafters. As these sound effects were not part of the script, they often proved more than disturbing to both actors and audience.

One night as we arrived at the theatre, we heard loud battering noises coming from the stairs at the side of the building. Investigating, we found one of the tenants armed with a baseball bat hammering at one of the rodents that was trying desperately to escape the savage blows. This rat hunter had a dozen dead rats lined up at the top of the stairs. He roused the rats one at a time; when the rat was cornered, he proceeded with the slaughter.

"I do this every once in a while," he said. "These God–damed rats are all over the place."

Although relieved to see these squeaking hecklers so effectively handled, we asked him to please refrain his activities until after our performance. He obliged for the sake of Art. He was an artist, too.

During that year, I added to my repertoire and now had about eight plays ready for performance. We stuck it out for most of the summer, but when the hot August days wafted the strong odors of the alley into our theatre, we began to lose patrons. The Depression was on, and the audiences were very small. So very reluctantly and sadly, giving up our somewhat historical location, we folded up our stage, packed up our actors, and moved out. Perhaps most of all, we were sorry to leave the friendly Italian barkeeper next door, who always supplied us with free coffee royals before each performance.

I needed some time to consider my next move and to take inventory of my accomplishments thus far. I had the opportunity to ship out for four months: a change of scene, first New York then the Orient, a hiatus badly needed.

Four months at sea afforded me the inspiration derived from new, strange places: the Philippines, Hawaii, China, and Japan. I made sketches of the crew, new peoples, lands, all far removed from the world on strings I had left behind. I thought of the many plays I would like to do and the many characters I wanted to create. It seemed inevitable that I would return to carry on what I had started out to do: explore theatre form with marionettes for adult audiences.

ELEVEN

... that your aim is not to become a celebrated actor, it is not to become the manager of a so-called successful theatre; it is not to become the producer of elaborate and much talked of plays; it is to become an artist of the theatre.

— *Craig,* On the Art of the Theatre

When I returned to San Francisco, I had no theatre and lacked the finances to set one up. At one time, I had worked with Reginald Travers, who had long been a director/producer/actor of San Francisco little theatre productions, occasionally designing sets for him. Upon arriving in the city, I discovered he had recently opened a small theatre in the Fairmont Hotel. He asked me if I would once again design settings for him.

"If you will help me, dear boy, perhaps we can work something out so that you can give special performances with your marionettes in my theatre."

The offer was tempting, but having no portable stage, I made other demands of him in exchange for designing his stage sets. I wanted to be cast in *Uncle Vanya* and *Richlieu*. He agreed. Reginald had many rich dowagers as his sponsors, and one of them asked me if I would give a special performance of *The Emperor Jones* with my marionettes in Reginald's theatre. It would be strictly invitational for her guests. She offered to provide me with a portable stage built to my specifications, an offer which I accepted with delight. It proved a gala occasion to which the cream of San Francisco society was invited. *Jones* was always a surefire success and won the praises of audience and sponsor.

Now that I had a portable stage, I could plan other shows. I built a new production of *Romeo and Juliet*. I made the marionettes in my studio and rehearsed my company in an empty store in the hotel. The settings were very modern, very simple semi-abstract forms which depended greatly on the lighting to achieve the romantic, tragic mood of the play. I used a flexible unit set with the addition of steps, low platforms, a balcony, and cut-out drops against a sky drop stretched in back of the back bridge. The marionettes were slender and graceful, moving with poetic gestures and yet responding with the dramatic action required in the duel scenes. I cut the play, keeping it within a reasonable playing time of less than two hours. It was a good choice for a marionette play. The beauty of Shakespeare's poetry came through in the passionate reading of the lines, backed up by the semi-abstract settings and colorful lighting.

Although the marionettes were costumed in traditional Renaissance style, the settings were not. They were strictly imaginative, designed for dramatic effect not realism. This combination always worked well with Shakespearean productions. A slavish attempt at realistic detail would only destroy the dramatic illusion that the marionettes themselves were able to convey.

Many problems arose in using double bridges made of folding stage parallel platforms, as they had to be stored in the limited storage room this small theatre could afford. Yet, in spite of the difficulties, we gave several productions in this theatre.

It sometimes seems a special providence has a way of solving the artist's problems. In this case, mine were solved by the benevolent Rabbi Weinstein, who asked me to put on two Bible plays for his synogogue. By chance, 718 Montgomery Street was again vacant at a rent of fifty dollars a month, a sum which Rabbi Weinstein advanced on the two shows. I was able to move in with the new stage and all of my characters, who had previously been uncomfortably housed in my basement.

I felt as though I had come home. I was back in the theatre where I had produced the first *Hamlet*. I wrote and prepared the two Biblical stories – *The Story of Esther* and *David and Goliath*, and the marionettes were back in business.

Although I now had a large portable marionette stage, lighting equipment, a switchboard, and record player, I had no desire to take shows out on the road. Touring and playing to schools and colleges were the means by which most puppeteers survived. I did very little of that. Instead, I stored the stage in back of the theatre and built a strong, permanent set of bridges of two feet by four feet which I found more comfortable. Here I could give my shows and add a new production every six to eight weeks. This suited me perfectly. The marionette theatre became an institution in San Francisco. Its uniqueness consisted in presenting a new kind of adult theatre to the habitués of San Francisco's Bohemia and Montgomery Street. The newspapers and columnists always gave us space. The marionettes were news.

The permanent marionette theatre has not always proved profitable for the average puppeteer. It requires preparing and building new shows while performing the current show for six or eight weeks. Special shows for children on Saturday afternoons must also be put on if the adult play is not suitable. But once a good–sized repertoire has been built up, it is more interesting to change plays at regular intervals than to play one show year in and year out, having to adapt equipment to all kinds of stages. The performances are always fresh and stimulating to both players and audiences, and the shows improve when they have been re–rehearsed and brought back after having been shelved for awhile. And, of course, there is the thrill of opening with a new show from time to time. If a new show didn't click, I could always revive an old standby. Even if a play didn't draw too well, I, at least, had the satisfaction of trying out something new. In this way, I also learned what would or would not go over.

The repertory marionette theatre has another distinct advantage over the travelling company: it allows the players the opportunity to play a wide range of different characters. The actor/puppeteer must develop new voices, sometimes several in one play, and ever increase his voice range. The puppeteer must always be able to play many different parts. He is never typecast, something the stage or picture actor cannot avoid.

A repertory theatre becomes a storehouse, not only of plays and an assortment of marionette characters, but also of units of scenery which the ingenious and inventive designer can adapt to different plays. I know of no better place to learn every phase of theatre–craft than the marionette theatre.

The return to Montgomery Street gave me new impetus. I planned new shows and went to work with renewed zeal. Jack Ford's *Iolanthe* gave me the idea of doing a Gilbert and Sullivan opera. I had nine plays now in repertoire in addition to *Romeo and Juliet,* and the two Biblical plays that I could run on Saturday matinees.

The Mikado seemed to me an ideal choice as the next production as it was possible to obtain complete recordings of the Doyle Carte production. The record player with a double turntable would make it possible to use two sets of records. As the dialogue was not recorded, the company could match the voices in the records to fill in between the musical numbers. We had no microphones in those days, but by projecting our voices, we were able to match the recorded sound. *The Mikado* proved to be an excellent selection, and it became one of our most popular shows.

For the costume and stage designs, I researched the old Japanese woodcuts. The characters were right out of the colorful prints of actors and actresses created by the great Japanese print makers. The characters were small, the heads carved like the ivory masks used in the Kabuki and Noe plays. Instead of fastening the screw eye to the neck and fitting it into the shoulder piece, I reversed the procedure, hollowing out the head at the jaw line and carving the neck as part of the shoulder piece. By putting the screw eye into the neck, I fitted it into the hollowed head, pinning it so that it moved like a little Japanese doll. The heads were painted like polished ivory masks. I fashioned the women's hairdresses out of black oil cloth, giving the effect of the elaborate stylized wigs they wore in the theatre.

The costumes were painted to provide the effect of the brocaded fabrics used in kimonos. I achieved the theatrical Japanese style of theatre instead of the usual comic opera style employed by the Savoyards. The results were more effective, yet lost none of the humorous aspect so essential to Gilbert and Sullivan.

During that season, I fitted in several other new productions. One was an adaptation of Wagner's *Siegfried*. The story, characters, and magnificent music seemed ideal for marionettes. It was an adult play with music that could also be given for young audiences on matinees.

There were few characters to build, and I would have the opportunity to create some exciting settings and characters. And the special effects would be challenging: the splitting of the anvil; the killing of the dragon; the wall of fire in the last act.

I was able to use the English libretto and worked in the recorded music throughout. The blond, athletic Siegfried was handsome in his bearskin costume as he battled Fafnir, the dragon, whom I made with a papier mâché head and movable jaws. Fafnir emerged only in part from his cave, revealing his long neck and clawed feet. When Siegfried gives Fafnir the mortal thrust with his sword, I produced the blood effect by means of a small balloon filled with red dye which squirted when depressed by a trigger arrangement. I achieved the wall of fire by hanging strips of colored gauze on a track under the back bridge, producing the effect of flames when moved in red and blue lights. Wagner's music, of course, aroused the dramatic, exciting mood the play needed. The opera worked exceedingly well as a marionette play and told the story better than the opera when performed in English. It is the kind of theatre marionettes do better than human actors and is another example of the wide range of theatre possible on a miniature stage where the artist is always in full control.

That season, I produced another play accompanied by music but of an entirely different nature. I found *Noël* in Paul McPharlin's *Repertory of Marionette Plays*. It was a Nativity play by Maurice Bouchor translated from the French by Paul McPharlin. The verse was beautiful. Against a sky drop with simple settings, the poetry was read to recorded choral and religious music by Bach, Handel, and Hayden. In the scenes where kings and animals file by, I used shadows. The characters were designed in the manner of Dresden figures, producing the effect of a crèche on display at Christmas time.

We kept our theatre well filled throughout the year in spite of the rather cramped quarters. Our audiences had to perch on makeshift seats, not the most comfortable, but they never complained and seemed to enjoy the novelty of this rather unique theatre.

TWELVE

The success of our marionette theatre enlarged our vision and we began to think of larger quarters. We wanted something more impressive than the narrow little store front at 718 Montgomery. Crawford Perks and Bob Southwick, my two assistants, Crawford's mother (who wanted a place to display her collection of antique furniture), and my wife, Jo, went out scouting for a new location. Crawford and Mrs. Perks finally located one on Clay Street between Polk and Van Ness. It had been built as a temporary church after the fire of 1906 and belonged to the Episcopal church at the corner. It had been used as a gymnasium, so it had a proper high ceiling; it also contained more than a hundred folding seats and was large enough so that Mrs. Perks could display her antiques. In addition, there were living quarters for her and her son. The price was one–hundred dollars per month, and Mrs. Perks agreed to share half the rent. Although it seemed an ideal arrangement, the location was far from the Montgomery Street Bohemia that had provided the marionettes with so much support in the past. But we decided to make the move in the hope of drawing larger audiences; 1749 Clay Street had a very impressive front entrance and was easily accessible to public transportation.

In March of 1933, after weeks of scrubbing, refurbishing, painting, decorating, hanging drapes, and setting up the stage, the Marionette Guild opened at its new location. Flyers and publicity had been sent out and posters distributed. As was my custom, I opened with *Hamlet*.

There was plenty of space: back stage, ceiling, workshop, and storage. The light was good, but the open spaces under the eaves made the auditorium drafty and cold. We heated it with kerosene stoves but also counted on the heat generated by the stage lights during performances.

With the number of plays in the repertoire, it was possible to change programs every six weeks, which allowed time for the preparation of new shows. I found that a sophisticated review type of program always drew audiences, so I prepared one, using a marionette George Bernard Shaw as Master of Ceremonies. It was written and played by Charles Bratt. Shaw came on to the music of Percy Grainger's "Country Gardens" and criticized each number in true Shavian style and wit. The program was made up of skits, musical numbers, and short plays, and included, among other things, Chekov's *The Marriage Proposal*, a soliloquy from Richard III, as recorded by John Barrymore, and original satirical sketches.

With many different types of marionettes on hand, I readapted some of them for the Variety Show. The material was always fresh, numbers could be changed, and new ones added on short notice. On one occasion, I made a small orchestra which played a recording of the overture to *The Marriage of Figaro* by Mozart, conducted by a marionette of Alfred Hertz, who was then conductor of the San Francisco Symphony.

I invited Alfred Hertz to a performance, and he was intrigued to see himself in miniature. The marionette, at the end of the number, withdrew his handkerchief to mop his brow, something Hertz never failed to do. The audience loved it. When Hertz came backstage after the performance, his only comment was: "Was I really as bad as that?"

I added several new plays during the 1934 season. The old melodrama of *Dr. Jekyll and Mr. Hyde* always fascinated me, and I remembered John Barrymore's chilling performance in the silent screen version. I had worked with a stock company in New Orleans, whose actor/producer, Ted Lorch, claimed to be the only actor to perform the play since Mansfield. It was a simple trick to make the transformation from Jekyll to Hyde and seemed a natural for marionettes. So I added the Robert Louis Stevenson classic to my repertoire. I included a note of mystery and modern stage craft in the horror story by designing the settings in the style of *The Cabinet of Dr. Caligary*, using shades of gray, black, and white in an exaggerated perspective, such as might be seen by the eye of a deranged mind. It worked perfectly. For the transformation, I used two marionettes, one for Jekyll and one for Hyde. Jekyll crouched behind a desk, bench, or lab table while, making horrible, convulsive sounds, Hyde appeared. For comedy relief, I added two policemen. Generally, I used the old stage version with only minor modifications. To the average puppeteer, *Dr. Jekyll and Mr. Hyde* may not seem exactly marionette material, but it worked.

To change the pace, I selected *Alice in Wonderland* as a following production. It had wide audience appeal and was always accepted as perfect marionette material. The version I used combined both *Alice* and *Through the Looking Glass,* one that had been played by Eva Le Gallienne's company in New York. So much material exists in both stories that I found it difficult to select the best parts to include in a script. Remo Bufano designed the masks and played a part in the New York production, keeping the character of the Tenniel drawings as his model, something I consider essential to a production of *Alice*.

The project was major as it required large heads and small bodies. The heads had to be modelled in clay, then molds made of plaster, and each head built inside the molds with papier mâché – a tedious process. The bodies, however, were carved of soft pine like my other marionettes. To achieve the Tenniel feeling in my costumes, I tailored them first in white muslin, and then with aniline dyes, I sketched the effect of the engravings, and added my colors.

My version of *Alice* was in two acts and called for many fast changes. While one scene played, another scene was set up behind it. As each scene ended, Alice walked through the wood to her next encounter, so that it was unnecessary to draw the curtain. The pieces of scenery were two–dimensional, cut out of plywood, and painted to give the effect of Tenniel's black and white pen drawings.

In addition to the arduous preparation, I painted the scenery hobbling around on one foot, having broken my ankle during a performance of *Emperor Jones*. But *Alice* proved a delightful show to perform. It was great fun playing many different characters, and there were many good parts for the other members of the company. It was a show of contrasts, paradoxes, peopled with creatures of a child's imagination – the kind of show in which puppeteers revel.

After the successful *Jekyll and Hyde*, I decided to do another old melodrama, one that had played a vital part in American history – and theatre history. As a play, Harriet Beecher Stowe's *Uncle Tom's Cabin* had been a popular stage piece with both touring and stock companies since the Civil War. It was internationally known and contained all the basic elements of theatre I looked for in a marionette play.

I obtained a copy of the old stage version which I cut to marionette size. In spite of the cutting, it still called for about fourteen scenes and fourteen characters. I designed it with painted roll drops and reversible wings – the style of the old road shows. We played it straight with no attempt at caricature. It possessed action, suspense, and good old–fashioned drama. There was Eliza, chased by blood hounds, crossing the ice (I used the old trick of the painted floor cloth draped on rockers to give the effect of the rushing river, with the ice floes). The full–sized Eliza crossed front stage, disappeared, followed by Haley, Marks, Tom Loker, and blood hounds. A small Eliza appeared in the distance as she reached the other side of the river. Comedy was provided by Little Eva, Topsy, and Aunt Ophelia. I used Dvorak's *New World Symphony* and Stephen Foster melodies as background music. The death scene of Little Eva was, of course, a tear jerker. The final tableau represented a bank of white clouds with Little Eva astride a white dove center, St. Clair and Uncle Tom on either side. As the dove carried Little Eva up to Heaven, the chorus sang "Goin' Home," a recording of a spiritual arranged from the *New World Symphony*.

After *Don Juan*, my favorite play by Molière is *L'Avare* (The Miser). It had also been one of my father's favorites, and I remembered his reading it to us in French when we were children. I wanted to play the part and decided to make it into a marionette play. It contained all the elements of *commedia dell'arte* which Molière used in so many of his plays. It depended largely on comic dialogue and situations which audiences did not appreciate as much as they did the material in some of my other plays. Nevertheless, I enjoyed playing the part of the cantankerous Harpagon, who accuses everyone of stealing his cash box.

L'Avare bore a definite resemblance to the old Italian comedies. While the old *commedia* was a spontaneous theatre which often played in public squares, Molière's comedies were carefully scripted in a style that was entirely classic. In this play, he satirized avarice, a common vice of his time, and attacked it by ridiculing his central character, Harpagon, a role he played himself. Molière developed a comic plot around the old man's vice. His son and daughter scheme against him with his housekeeper and make a fool of him as he seeks the hand of a beautiful young woman, who is in love with his son. They defeat his plan to marry off his daughter to a rich old man, a match which the old miser considered advantageous as there no dowry involved. The son and his servant steal the miser's hidden cash box, promising to return it if he will consent to the marriages of the son and his sister to their respective sweethearts.

I designed the single setting in the 17th Century style of the period. It served as the background for the characters who were dressed in the traditional wigs and costumes of the time.

Shakespeare's *The Merchant of Venice* and Gilbert and Sullivan's *Pinafore* were the two other productions included in that season's list of plays. My purpose had been to offer a season of marionette plays that differed from the puppet programs usually offered and to illustrate that a wide range of material can be successfully performed by marionettes. For some reason, neither of these plays appealed to my audiences as did my other Shakespearean productions or *The Mikado*.

THIRTEEN

The Readiness is all.

— Shakespeare, *Hamlet* – V:2

The height of the Depression brought an end to The Marionette Guild. I had learned a great deal about marionettes during the years I had devoted to building up a repertory of plays. I had tested them in all of the theatrical forms accepted as belonging strictly to live theatre. I had avoided realistic contemporary material, realizing it as rarely suited to my purpose. Quite early, I had discovered that any attempt to reduce the photographic image of man to the size of a marionette two feet tall would be wasted effort, defeating the function of the marionette. Primarily, I dealt with theatre, albeit a miniature one, in which the characters, although not real, suggested reality. An abstract or semi–abstract figure can appear more real on the marionette stage than an actor on a large stage.

The larger–than–life figures, that have been used in some productions, are merely huge masks moved by a human body. While visually and dramatically related to the marionette, they do not compare to the illusion created by a jointed, stringed puppet manipulated by a puppeteer. To reveal everything is to destroy the magic. I have always subscribed to James Whistler's theory: "A work of art is complete when the means whereby it is accomplished is thoroughly eliminated." The larger the mask, the more obvious are the materials used in making it. It is more static than a marionette and belongs to the art of mime or the dance.

One of the definitions of illusion given in the dictionary reads: "a perception of a thing which misrepresents it, or gives it qualities not present in reality." Those qualities not present in reality are the very qualities I found I was able to present through the medium of puppetry – in my case, the marionette. Size was not a problem; it actually proved advantageous to use an instrument of miniature size. Larger–than–life figures would have defeated my purpose as I was able to achieve the effect of larger–than–life by theatrical means. And theatre was my object – theatrical illusion. It is this that brings into exercise the imagination of the audience, the element necessary to arrive at a perfect performance.

Finally, to sum up the many advantages of the marionette repertory theatre, I wish to point out the wide experience afforded the marionette producer in creating many different kinds of shows. As he is always in production, he consequently develops a style in making marionettes for various types of plays. Indulging his own tastes in the selection of plays, he has the opportunity to study varying audience reactions to what he presents. If he plays to children of different age groups and his shows are well done, he is on safe ground. Audiences will seek him out. On the other hand, if he presents sophisticated plays for adults such as classic works, he will have to develop an audience. This audience may, at first, be skeptical of the seriousness of the effort. The marionette can always provoke its viewers to laughter, but can it move them to tears, to feelings of deep emotion? The answer is "yes." It is up to the actor.

FOURTEEN

It was the best of times, it was the worst of times – the spring
of hope and the winter of despair.

— Charles Dickens, *A Tale of Two Cities*

Although 1934 marked the end of The Marionette Guild, we
knew that to have survived until that time in the midst of worldwide
economic devastation was an accomplishment in itself. It also prepared me for the Federal Theatre Project which began in 1936.

In that year, Roosevelt's administration created the Works Progress Administration that put into action a vast national program to
provide work for unemployed artists, musicians, actors, vaudevillians,
dancers, and puppeteers. The arts program of the WPA was in addition to the other work programs already in progress. Its intention was
to find jobs for people not necessarily to promote national art.

In January of that year, the Federal Theatre Project started, including puppetry as one of the performing arts. I was selected to head
the San Francisco unit and was later made Supervisor of Puppetry for
the State of California.

The prospect was exciting. Puppeteers were put to work and their
efforts subsidized by the government. I was given a freehand in or-
ganizing the unit; a budget was set up for necessary materials, and I
could hire my own staff. Work space and a theatre were provided.
Anyone on relief was eligible to apply for jobs, and a few on non–relief were also allowed to be hired if special skills were required. To be
eligible for relief, one must be unemployed with no other source of
income.

I started out with fifteen people, most of whom were unskilled in
puppetry. Usually, the women could sew, and the men had some
experience with tools. Those who could carve, paint, or had some
stage experience readily adapted to the construction of marionettes
and were easily trained as puppeteers. In addition, two writers were
assigned to us.

51

At our first meeting, we discussed material for our first production. It was suggested that the Irish story, *The Crock of Gold*, by James Stephens would appeal to both children and adults. It had been done in New York by Meyer Levin, but our two writers were assigned to write an original version.

The story concerns the legendary crock of gold belonging to the leprechauns who live in a cave beneath a tree. Their gold is stolen, and they plan revenge on the thief. They steal the washboard of Meehawl McMurrahu's wife and kidnap the two children of two old philosophers. They make Caitilin, Meehawl's beautiful daughter, fall in love with the god Pan and eventually have her taken by the Irish god, Angus Og. We cut the story to play in ten scenes, using twenty-four characters.

I designed all of the characters and settings and put the group to work. They showed great enthusiasm and quickly became completely absorbed in the project. On the technical side, we had the assistance of stage carpenters, electricians, scene painters, and sound men.

The carpenters built a portable stage and the electricians rigged up a small switchboard with dimmers. The stage was completely equipped with lights, backdrop, side wings, and curtains. The two bridges provided ample room for the full company. We also had adequate sound equipment with microphones and a record player.

A small theatre above a night club on Bush Street was rented by the Federal Theatre to start off the program. It was also the headquarters for the project headed by Elizabeth Elson. We were given workshop space upstairs where we built the marionettes. I carved all the heads and trained the crew in carving and assembling the bodies. The women made the costumes, while in the shop downstairs, the carpenters and scene painters carried out the settings from my drawings.

While construction went on, we scheduled rehearsals, and I worked with the actors to develop their Irish dialects. All lines were memorized, and when the stage was ready, the company was trained in manipulation. Once the marionettes had been strung, the rehearsals began in earnest. After three months of intensive work, the *Crock of Gold* was ready for the opening performance, the first Federal Theatre production to play in San Francisco. It was a great accomplishment for this group of people, many of whom had never held a marionette before coming on the project.

I had a revolving stage constructed to speed up the many scene changes required by the play. We opened to enthusiastic first nighters and ran for several months. By the time the live stage plays were ready, we had a well-trained company of puppeteers who each earned the eighty-seven dollars a month paid to the relief workers. It was another month before the actors on the main project were ready to perform their first play.

In the months that followed, I revived my own production of *Alice*, with new settings cut out of plywood, again using the revolving stage to speed up scene changes. Later, I used my original marionettes in a revival of *The Mikado*, which gave the company time to build a Variety Show.

Instead of using a stage curtain in this production of *The Mikado*, I had a pair of large screens built and stretched with translucent drafting cloth that opened like sliding screens in a Japanese house. When the overture began, the lights on stage gradually came up on dimmers as the house lights went out. The settings appeared like a large watercolor when the sliding screens opened slowly, revealing the chorus on stage. A beautiful effect resulted – like an old Japanese print coming to life.

The Variety Show was not the usual collection of vaudeville acts expected of marionettes but included such numbers as a reading of Poe's *The Raven*, acted out by a marionette of Edgar Allen Poe in a constructivist–type setting against the sky drop. The reading built up to a dramatic climax as the prophetic raven flew in and settled on the bust of Pallas Athene over the door. Another effective number was created when a symphony orchestra appeared as moving shadows with a marionette of Leopold Stokowski conducting on a podium. The shadows appeared as moving abstract forms with a brilliant kaleidoscopic effect of color. The moving cutouts represented the different instruments in the orchestra as they dominated certain passages. Disney's scouts must have seen the production when it played in Los Angeles, as the same idea was used in the film "Fantasia."

I used acrobats, singers, tap dancers, and a chorus of the Dionne Quintuplets, very popular at the time, to fill out the program. These were fitted in between such numbers as a recording of John Barrymore's soliloquy from *Richard III*. There were dramatic sketches, including Chekov's *The Marriage Proposal*, and an original skit, a satire on prison life, written on the project.

A new production of *The Emperor Jones* was built on the project and played first at the old Columbia Theatre and later at the Alcazar, both theatres having been leased by the Federal Theatre. All the productions were well received and did better business at the box office than some of the legitimate shows.

By the end of the first year, our marionettes had done so well that I was appointed State Director of Puppetry for California. This took me to Los Angeles where I directed activities for both units, sending productions back and forth.

When I arrived in Los Angeles in 1937, Bob Bromley was director of the unit. Fifty people were on the project, making up a company of varied talents capable of developing different kinds of shows. Unfortunately, it was difficult for them to conform to my tastes, and I ran into a lot of opposition from the company.

One man in the group was a skilled special–effects man, who had worked in films for years; another was a fine wood carver and sculptor, who invented complicated ball–and–socket joints for the marionette bodies that did not always respond to simple manipulation. The women were very good at making every kind of costume and worked tediously to carry out my designs. One of them was an expert in animal making and, in one instance, took three months to build Rosinante, Don Quixote's horse. She carried out such minute details as making the horse's teeth move when its mouth opened. The eyeballs rolled, the bony shanks protruded, and you could count every rib in the body. It was near perfection mechanically and carried out Cervante's description of the Don's horse as no real horse could have done. However, a simpler construction would have achieved the same effect.

The objective of the program was to keep everyone busy with the aim of producing adult shows, as well as children's shows designed above their usual level of taste. The puppeteers, those who performed, were better manipulators than actors, concentrating on the former rather than on dramatics. They could put a tap dancer through his paces with expertise but were unable to make a reading of Edgar Allen Poe's *The Raven* come to life or provide the characteristic impudence requisite of George Bernard Shaw. Their greatest contribution to the project was the building of a truck stage which they took around to every Los Angeles playground, as well as many schools. The program consisted of clowns, dancers, chorus girls, tap dancers, and a few trick marionettes, a program to which they gave their best efforts as it was their kind of show.

In 1938, the Federal Theatre was assigned to prepare several programs to be given at the Golden Gate International Exposition on Treasure Island in San Francisco Bay. The island had been made of fill–in land and became the famous Treasure Island on which the Exposition was built. The Federal Theatre and the Marionette Theatre were housed in the Federal Building and both were designed with the most modern stage and lighting equipment available. Our theatre had a specially designed revolving stage with a balcony level. The scenery was built in complete units which were put in place while the scenes were played. In the case of *Snow White and the Seven Dwarfs,* a show prepared for the Exposition, the Dwarfs marched from one scene to the next as the stage revolved. The music for *Snow White* was composed and recorded on the project.

When the Exposition opened in the early Spring of 1939, the company had been moved to San Francisco and housed in a hotel. The San Francisco company prepared *Rip Van Winkle*; the marionettes were made in Los Angeles. The Los Angeles company prepared *Snow White* and a new Variety Show, thus giving us three alternating productions. We gave four performances daily and were quite an attraction at the Fair.

With all the effort put into these programs and the enthusiasm with which they were received, we felt reasonably sure we would remain at the Exposition for its duration. However, without warning, when the Fair was at its peak attendance in July, 1939, Congress suddenly closed all Federal Theatres. We were sent back to Los Angeles, and what we had hoped would become a nationally subsidized theatre was abruptly ended. The reason given was that the projects had become subversive.

As the Fair continued, the Recreation Project of the WPA took over the theatre, and in 1940, I returned to Treasure Island as head of a new company. I created a very colorful production of *Pinocchio*, that played until the end of the Exposition.

In 1941, when all of the arts projects were terminated, we were all put into war training classes. During the war years, my marionette activities ceased, and I went to work in a shipyard.

After World War II, it was not economically feasible to reopen my theatre. The times had changed, and the audiences seemed to have changed with them. Real estate was too expensive to allow me to find a location, and the interest in puppetry was eclipsed by other entertainment forms. I taught a class in adult–educational puppetry for a brief period. I could still find actors who enjoyed the experience, but we had to perform under the sponsorship of organizations like the Junior League. Out of this came an elaborate production of Dickens' *Oliver Twist* that I adapted from an old stage version. I used students who ranged in age from fourteen to fifty–five. I made costume drawings from the Cruikshank engravings. I assigned the settings to a young stage designer. They were effective, but I found them lacking the spirit which I would have imparted to them.

In all of my earlier experiences, I worked with people who had no previous puppetry experience. I taught them understanding and respect for legitimate theatre. I worked on the delivery of their lines, how to develop character voices, and how to feel the vibrations they sent down through the moving instrument below. I made them avoid trick manipulation and taught them to suit the action to the words as they brought the marionettes to life through their readings. They experienced the impact of this on the audience and derived the satisfaction an actor has when on stage, providing a natural exercise to the audience's imagination. I always found these elements inspiring to those with whom I worked. They ignited forces that produced artistic productions that convinced audiences that they had been involved in unique theatrical experiences.

Teaching college classes in puppetry, I discovered the major interest to be in craftsmanship and much less in the theatrical possibilities and achievements of the puppet. This period of work at San Francisco State College proved the beginning of a hard reevaluation of my life with marionettes.

FIFTEEN

Get used to thinking that there is nothing. Nature loves nothing so well as to change existing forms and to make new ones like them.

— Marcus Aurelius Antoninus

When television began expanding to local programming in the fifties, I believed it would prove a boon to puppetry. It would, hopefully, find use for the puppets in the new medium in addition to offering some financial security in the field. This would also bring about the development of new techniques and provide the means of presenting puppetry to large audiences. As it turned out, with few exceptions, this was a somewhat unrealistic dream.

Full of expectation, a few colleagues and I hoped to make a killing by getting in on the ground floor. Entirely ignorant of the technical demands of television, we decided to crash the gates. Peter Abenheim, a writer, had the same idea. We teamed up, breaking in on the scene with scripts and marionettes, hoping to tantalize the station managers who were searching for new material. We talked them into giving us several auditions with no significant results and no takers. We did have the experience of appearing before the cameras, only to discover it would not be an easy job. We then went our separate ways: he landing a spot as a storyteller, using a puppet which I had made for him, and I doing a few commercials with marionettes. During the holidays, I put on shows for department stores in order to pay the studio rent.

In 1951, the studios depended on staff announcers to carry on interview programs using any and everyone who would sit down and talk before the cameras. This was done for free publicity. The stations were looking for sponsors, and the latter were scarce. National advertisers were few and far between, and local advertisers were not convinced television would pay off. In order to keep the stations running, they carried a few inexpensive sustaining programs that were carried on by the staff.

Interview programs seemed popular at a time when those who owned TV sets watched anything on the air and all stations used them. I auditioned first with a marionette spoof on the new programs, a sacred institution not to be made fun of. Then I came up with an interview program, fifteen minutes twice weekly, which ABC accepted. I called it *Willie and the Baron*, the Baron being Baron Woodley, an interviewer of storybook characters, and Willie, his stooge office boy. It was novel and appealed to children and adults as an afternoon program. Lettie Connell, my son Dion, and I put on the two weekly programs. The Baron invited well-known characters from nursery rhymes, folk tales, historical works, and many from popular classics, such as: Alice (*Alice in Wonderland*), Long John Silver (*Treasure Island*), Three Blind Mice, Punch and Judy, the Red and White Queens (*Alice*), Humpty Dumpty, Sherlock Holmes and Dr. Watson, and many others. The list of possibilities was endless, and the job of preparing and adapting the marionettes from my stockpile was time consuming. I also had to think up and write two scripts each week. But we were on television, that magic box that eventually found its way into every household, that magic box that had to be fed and consumed material like crazy.

We would arrive at the studio, the old Sutro mansion atop Twin Peaks (the first ABC station in San Francisco) which had been converted into a makeshift telecasting operation, KGO, with scripts and suitcases stuffed with marionettes. We operated from a single bridge in an office setting that included a picture window and photo mural of the Golden Gate and Sutro Forest. Hanging in front of the bridge, at eye level, was the stand on which we clipped the script. We had one run-through before going on the air, flipping pages as we read the dialogue and manipulated the marionettes. There were always the comic situations involving the excitable office boy and guests with gags related to the original story. It proved amusing and novel, albeit somewhat primitive in that we had no rehearsal time to carry out minute detail.

After that, I tackled anything that came along: puppets for advertising agencies, beer commercials, a series for Calso Water. Trying to please sponsors and account executives proved frustrating and required endless conferences and stacks of sketches. Then there was the problem of pleasing the film photographers who regarded marionettes as strange little monsters who were not always on cue, whose lip-sink and timing demanded many takes. Playing *Hamlet* with marionettes had not prepared me for this. I was now in a commercial field that made strict demands on puppets and puppeteers. It was a whole new ball game. In filming the movable mouth of a small marionette, it was necessary to move with split-second timing and on cue. The mouth was controlled by a single string, the opening and closing of which was accomplished by a trigger action in the center of the control. It often required many takes to satisfy the photographers, who wanted perfect synchronization of mouth articulation to the taped voice.

Not until I went into television did I find it necessary to use movable mouths. The bodies, too, differed from the slender classic figures I had used in dramatic shows. The heads and bodies were larger and heavier. To develop a mouth that could be opened and closed with string action, I had to make larger heads made of plastic wood. They were first modeled in clay, then cast in plaster that was lined with plastic wood. The mouth had to be cut out, counter-weighted, fitted, and pinned into place. All parts had to be sanded and smoothed so that the joint moved easily. To serve the puposes of television, my classic marionette gave way to the more conventional, commercial type of figure. I continued to use carved bodies. The painting of the heads had to be more finished as the cameras picked up every detail in the close-ups.

After six months on the air, KGO cancelled *Willie and the Baron*. We had failed to attract sponsors. Despite this, I was not discouraged. I had gotten my foot in the door. Although this was certainly not Shakespeare, a whole new field was opening up for the marionettes. I now had to learn something about selling the product, pleasing advertisers, account executives, and art directors of the agencies, as well as the sponsor who had the final word on his commercial. Sponsors who knew nothing about marionettes, considered them as a novel way of giving a sales pitch.

What had happened to my beautiful dream of a classic marionette theatre? It had been sacrificed to the needs of that great commercial dragon who gobbled up or threw aside ideas and material not considered acceptable to the vast buying public wooed by this new medium. Survival was now the name of the game, and the sponsor the "angel" to look for and cater to if I was to stay in business. Now, it was business before art. This was the compromise I had to make. This was my lost freedom. I found myself plunged into commercialism in art, that which I had always denounced, forced by the necessity of finding a market for my marionettes.

SIXTEEN

The time has come, the Walrus said,
　　To talk of many things
Of Shoes – and ships – and sealing wax –
　　Of cabbages and kings
And why the sea is boiling hot –
　　And whether pigs have wings.

— Lewis Carroll

In the Spring of 1952, a sponsor unexpectedly loomed on the horizon. A lady from The Latham Foundation for the Promotion of Humane Education, whose headquarters were in Oakland, came to me with an idea for a television program for children. The Foundation had developed a monthly bulletin that featured a little cartoon character called "Brother Buzz." He was a bumble bee dressed in top hat and tails, whose mission it was to promote a better understanding between man and animals. The Foundation slogan read: "Be Kind to Every Living Creature."

This very kind lady asked me if it would be possible to develop Brother Buzz as a marionette for television. He was the brainchild of a little old lady who had written a series of stories about a bumble bee and his experiences in man's world. I read some of the stories and considered the proposition. Since I was now in the business of marionettes for television and had no other commitments, I accepted the assignment. It was to be a weekly fifteen minute program, and I was to use the material already written in story form.

After scripting the stories, I found the series would require the making of various animals, insects, birds – nearly every species in the animal kingdom. Undaunted, I submitted the first scripts, which were happily accepted, and sketches of some of the characters. I made my bid, and the shows were scheduled to begin in the Fall of 1952, which gave me about four months for preparation. We reached an agreeable financial arrangement (that is always important in television deals), signed the contract, and began my series that was to remain fourteen years on the air.

The Westinghouse station was to present it as a public service program. The Latham Foundation was to pay the cost of production. KPIX scheduled it for an afternoon telecast and provided a live emcee who introduced Brother Buzz and gave the Foundation's pitch of being kind to animals and climbing the "Steps to the Castle of World Friendship." It first appeared as a live show; these were the early days of video–broadcasting, before the advent of sound tape or video tape.

Since these stories were principally for children, it seemed logical to Mrs. X, who wrote the stories, to begin the series in Elfland. In the first program, the Elf King selects one of his elves as his ambassador to the animal kingdom. He transforms him into a bumble bee, donned in top hat and tails, and renames him "Brother Buzz." He begins by becoming acquainted with different species of bees and meets "Busy Bee," who becomes his constant companion in his many adventures.

I realized that a bumble bee flying from place to place had to do it on camera, so I designed a revolving stage made of duraluminum pipes that could be folded up and rolled into a corner of the studio, thereby eliminating the need to set it up each week between shows. When on camera, Brother Buzz and Busy Bee had to fly from one set to another, the turntable was moved by the floormen to the next location. The settings, such as trees, bushes, rocks, and one special hollow tree trunk that served as Brother Buzz's official dwelling, were built in unit pieces. The tree trunk served as the starting point for most of the programs.

As the big problem involved providing different characters for each week's story, I established a number of stock characters who reappeared in different programs. The Owl, the Raccoon, the Blue Jay, the Bear, and many others were humanized. They brought their problems to Brother Buzz who tried to solve them. To satisfy my sponsor, I had to write special programs for "Be Kind to Animals Week," "National Dog Week," and holidays such as Easter, Halloween, Groundhog Day, Christmas, etc. To relate all of these occasions to the animal world was not always easy since the elderly lady (a cantankerous secretary) controlled all the material that went into the scripts. She had the power to pass or reject every script before it went on the air and often made last minute demands and changes that were frustrating. I was responsible for the construction of the animal marionettes, a job that quite taxed my ingenuity. These animals varied from the peculiar structure of a praying mantis to the awkward bulk of an elephant or walrus. I had to approximate the movements of each, making their movements convincing and finding character voices that suited their peculiar characteristics.

One of the sponsor's ideas was to have Brother Buzz travel to foreign countries to meet those animals native to, for example, Mexico, Africa, Australia, India, South America, and, on one occasion, to Alaska to meet the polar bear and walrus. I also had to provide changes of costume to suit the locale. Buzz and Busy Bee traveled by plane, rocket, or the back of a bird, and, in one instance, were transported by the North Wind. As my marionette menagerie enlarged, it grew to include every type of living creature from an insect larvae to a kangaroo. Every possible kind of material went into the making of these creatures. Some bodies were made of chicken wire covered with foam rubber, the legs and arms carved of wood. The parts of the marionettes were covered with skins, fake fur, or whatever suggested the proper texture. The hard shells of an alligator or an armadillo called for combinations of cloth, papier mâché, and, sometimes, plastic wood. When I took on the assignment, I hadn't realized I would have to become some kind of taxidermist. I surprised myself with the new creations I produced each week. I spent as much time researching as I did building, at the same time learning about nature, ecology, and the rights of animals.

For eight years we were on KPIX, Channel 5. During that time, we were given a Peabody Award for outstanding service as an educational program. My son, Dion, played Brother Buzz, Lettie Connell played Busy Bee, and I played all the other odd characters. We evolved from the live telecast to the prerecorded sound tape, manipulating to the playback, then to sound tape and video tape, all prerecorded for later telecasting. Lettie was offered an opportunity to create her own show and for a period was replaced by Virginia Arnett and later Marian Derby. We became part of a segment of the Captain Fortune program on KPIX, with the ubiquitous Peter Abenheim, then moved to Captain Satellite's program on KTVU, Channel 2, Oakland.

After eight years, Dion left the program and my younger son, Bruce, whose voice is similar to Dion's, took over. The program continued for six more years. Many changes occurred over these years. We graduated from tape to film and were syndicated over forty–eight stations. The filmed programs were expanded to an half–hour with fifteen minutes of integrated live documentary. This eventually usurped the program and destroyed the original quality of the early all–marionette series. *Buzz* carried on until 1967, when the series was cancelled by the Foundation as a result of a change of secretary. The films have been converted to video tape and are frequently shown on the Oakland educational channel. *Brother Buzz* is still alive and well.

In 1957, I was asked by the San Francisco Symphony orchestra director, Enrique Jorda, to collaborate in doing the puppets for De Falla's *Master Peter's Puppet Show*. Lettie assisted me with the puppets and performance. I designed the puppets as large, primitive

Catalan types and integrated them with live mime performers of Don Quixote and the peasants. The orchestra was placed on one side of the stage, the large puppet stage on the other. Designed as a chamber opera, the puppets appear in the booth of Master Pedro where they are ultimately attacked by Don Quixote in one of his hallucinatory spells. I constructed the large figures with heads of papier mâché, so they would carry the great distance of the San Francisco Opera House.

That same year, at the National Puppetry Festival held at the University of California, Los Angeles, Blanding Sloan and I once more collaborated in a new production of *The Emperor Jones*. Our object was to recreate the spirit of our 1928 production. Dion assisted me in playing Smithers and reciting the Congo prologue. That was the first opportunity the membership of the Puppeteers of America had had to witness one of my productions. Being now something of a legend, I wanted to see if my theories were still effective. With disappointment, I received the rather damp reaction of this group. They had come with the critical eye of the puppeteer not as the open-minded audience who wants to witness an exciting theatrical production. They felt that the puppets were not cleverly manipulated, that the play was not puppet material, and that the performance was too powerful for the puppets to encompass. I decided it was time to stop this kind of work.

It was not until 1979 that I made my final attempt to produce what I believed was an exciting and convincing theatrical endeavor. My son, Bruce, had never had the opportunity to work with me in a classical production. He had devoted his considerable talent to educational puppetry, but the desire to do Shakespeare with marionettes had always excited him. Although I had begun to sell many of my figures to collectors, I had found time to create a cast of *Macbeth*. These puppets were somewhat larger than the original cast of 1929.

Bruce had met a young Canadian, Doug Laird, at one of the festivals, who expressed a desire to put up the finances for a full-scale production of a classic with my marionettes. With this incentive, I went ahead, designed and built sets, completed the cast, and waited while Bruce found a place to put on the production. Dion had agreed to stage the play and make the cuts. He also played several parts, cast the actors, and selected the music.

Due to the generosity of Father James Dempsey, we were finally offered the facilities of the University of San Francisco Drama Department. We used their auditorium, lights, and technicians. Bruce had arranged with the Academy of Sciences, which was hosting the travelling Shakespeare exhibit from Folger Library in Washington, D.C. to put on *Macbeth* as part of the exhibition

We first tried out the production at the University of San Francisco, then moved the entire production to the Hall of Sciences. I participated with my sons by playing Duncan and my old role of the Porter. Bruce gave a masterly performance as Macbeth. He had also supervised the building of the new stage, constructed especially for this production, handled the printing of the posters and publicity, and made the contacts necessary to get the production on the boards.

We played for a week at the Academy. The production was most enthusiastically received. I was gratified by the unsolicited praise of a visiting drama professor from a South Carolina university, who said it was the most moving production of *Macbeth* he had ever seen. Once again, and for the last time, I felt that the play was the thing. The lines created the power that was imparted to my figures. The audience was once again taken out of itself by the power of imaginative involvement. Approaching my eightieth year, I felt quite sincerely: "our revels now are ended."

ENVOI

The tendency toward the natural has nothing to do with Art
and is abhorrent when it is shown in Art.

— Craig, *Art of Theatre*

Over a period of nearly fifty years, my marionettes evolved from
a classic form, free from any restrictions or dictates by anyone other
than myself, into one that necessitated satisfying the requirements of
a sponsor and a television station. I started out with a guinea pig –
Hamlet – and ended up with *Brother Buzz*, a television personality
who managed to survive fourteen years in the most intensely competi-
tive of all the performing arts. I sacrificed some of that precious freedom I enjoyed in the earlier years but managed to maintain certain
standards and continued as the artist in control. I did not resort to
naturalness but reshaped nature to serve my own ends. I succeeded
in circumventing the many road blocks along the way. During those
fourteen years, *Brother Buzz* found an audience of children who
communicated with him by joining his club, writing him letters, and
sending him drawings. Sometimes the "message of kindness" was a
bit saccharine, but he was real to his young viewers, as were all the
varied creatures who shared his program.

Though contemporary puppets have taken on new shapes, new
personalities, and now reach millions, the power of the figure brought
to life by his human creator is still more believable than his human
competitors and gives new exercise to the human imagination.

It seems, then, that the marionette, born into a human world of
chaos, struggle, and conflict, a world inflicted with a flesh and blood
supreme superiority that breeds intolerance and hatred, and battles
vainly against a mortality as inevitable as the rising and setting of the
sun, continues to emerge serene and unperturbed by all that tran-
spires around him. He is Man's soul and Man's conscience. He pro-
claims Man's virtues and attacks Man's vices yet remains free from
contamination. He plays at war without spilling a drop of blood; he

beheads his enemies without causing them discomfort; he preaches and moralizes in a transgressive world and suffers little more than the penalty of being silenced for his crime.

If he is cast out of the theatre, he takes up his stand on the nearest street corner. If the law forces him to move on, he takes to the open road. If he loses prestige, he manages to retain that which is more important: his freedom and in the face of the most harrowing experiences, he always retains his sense of humor. He is endowed with Man's immortal soul – a free, uncompromising, self–justifying, imperishable soul embodied in a block of wood, moved by strings, and set in motion by the will of Man.

BIBLIOGRAPHY

Boehn, Max Von. *Dolls and Puppets*. Philadelphia: David McKay, 1932. New edition issued by Charles T. Branford Co., Newton Centre, Massachusetts, 1956. Reprint. Cooper Square Publishers, New York.

Craig, Edward Gordon. *On the Art of The Theatre*. New York: Theatre Arts Books.

Joseph, Helen Haiman. *A Book of Marionettes*. New York: Viking Press, 1929.

McIsaac, F.J. *The Tony Sarg Marionette Book*, Illustrated by Tony Sarg. New York: B.W. Huebsch. Inc., 1921. Reprint. Viking Press, 1940.